access to history

Stalin's Russia 1924–53

Michael Lynch

HODDER
EDUCATIO
PART OF HACHETTE LIV

In memory of Catherine May Burns Sweeney (1915–2001)

Study guides updated, 2008, by Sally Waller (AQA) and Angela Leonard (Edexcel).

The Publishers would like to thank the following for permission to reproduce copyright material:

Photo credits

p.38 © Bettman/Corbis; **pp.68, 72** David King Collection; **p.120** Poster Collection, RU/SU 650, Hoover Institution Archives; **pp.13, 20** © Hulton-Deutsch collection/Corbis; **p.86** Solo Syndication/Associated Newspapers

Every effort has been made to trace all copyright holders, but if any have been inadvertently overlooked the Publishers will be pleased to make the necessary arrangements at the first opportunity.

Hachette Livre UK's policy is to use papers that are natural, renewable and recyclable products and made from wood grown in sustainable forests. The logging and manufacturing processes are expected to conform to the environmental regulations of the country of origin.

Orders: please contact Bookpoint Ltd, 130 Milton Park, Abingdon, Oxon OX14 4SB. Telephone: (44) 01235 827720. Fax: (44) 01235 400454. Lines are open 9.00–5.00, Monday to Saturday, with a 24-hour message answering service. Visit our website at www.hoddereducation.co.uk

Cover photo: State Russian Museum, St. Petersburg, Russia/The Bridgeman Art Library
Illustrations by Derek Griffin
Typeset in New Baskerville 10/12pt by GreenGate Publishing Services, Tonbridge, Kent
Printed in Malta

A catalogue record for this title is available from the British Library

ISBN: 978 0340 965 894

Contents

Dedication

Keith Randell (1943–2002)

The *Access to History* series was conceived and developed by Keith, who created a series to 'cater for students as they are, not as we might wish them to be'. He leaves a living legacy of a series that for over 20 years has provided a trusted, stimulating and well-loved accompaniment to the post-16 study. Our aim with these new editions is to continue to offer students the best possible support for their studies.

1

Lenin's Russia, 1917–24 – the Nation that Stalin Inherited

POINTS TO CONSIDER

Joseph Stalin dominated the Soviet Union for more than a quarter of a century from the mid-1920s to his death in 1953. He was one of the most extraordinary men of his time, making a huge impact on his nation and on the world. Yet his achievements, for good or bad, grew out of prepared soil. It was because he was heir to Lenin and the Russian Revolution that Stalin was able to do what he did. That is why it is necessary as a first step in analysing Stalin's Russia to examine the situation in the Soviet Union as it was at the time of Lenin's death in 1924. It was this situation that Stalin exploited to make himself master of the Soviet nation that Lenin had begun to shape. This chapter examines:

- Lenin's exercise of power, 1917–24
- Soviet society under Lenin
- Lenin's legacy.

Key dates

1917	February Revolution
	October Revolution
1917–24	Consolidation of Bolshevik power
1918	Decree separating Church and State
1918–20	Russian Civil War
	Foreign interventions
	The Red Terror
1921	Ban on factionalism
1922	Purges and show trials
1923	Lenin's Testament
1924	Death of Lenin

1 | Lenin in Power, 1917–24

The October Revolution, 1917

The pivotal moment in Lenin's shaping of Russia was the October Revolution in 1917. This was the event which was to become legendary. Using the agency of the **Soviets**, Lenin's **Bolsheviks** had overthrown the **Provisional Government** which had ruled Russia since the **February Revolution** eight months earlier.

Lenin and the Bolsheviks then claimed that their triumph gave them an absolute right to govern Russia. In their eyes, their success in the October Revolution validated their belief that they were an unstoppable force of history with every right to shape the new Russia as they saw fit. This was not merely a political boast. As **Marxists**, the Bolsheviks believed that they truly represented the will of the Russian **proletariat** who, in accordance with the scientific laws of the **dialectic**, had now taken power.

However, when the Bolsheviks took over in Russia in 1917 they faced enormous tasks. Whatever their grand claims, they were in reality a small party trying to impose their authority on Russia and facing fierce opposition within the nation and from outside. Yet, seven years later, by the time of Lenin's death in 1924, the Bolsheviks had overcome all the major challenges to their authority and had transformed Russia into the **USSR**. This involved their fighting and winning a desperate civil war (1918–20) against their political opponents, successfully resisting a series of foreign interventions and surviving a succession of severe economic crises.

Lenin's methods of government

The consolidation of Bolshevik power was a remarkable achievement, but it was gained only by using the most ruthless and violent means. Lenin had allowed no opposition to his government. During the **Red Terror**, political enemies had been crushed and critics within the Party suppressed. Lenin's years in power left the Soviet Union with a tradition of authoritarian rule and terror. There were also serious economic problems that had still to be solved if the USSR was to survive as a nation.

Democratic centralism

Although Lenin rejected the Russian past, he remained very much its heir. He had as little time for genuine democracy as the tsars had. The rule of the Bolsheviks was a continuation of the absolutist tradition in Russia. The Civil War and foreign interventions, by intensifying the threat to the Bolshevik government, provided it with the excuse for demanding total conformity from the masses and the Party as the price of the Revolution's survival. Bolshevik control was intended to be absolute. The events of 1917 did not mark a complete break with the past. Rather they were the replacement of one form of state authoritarianism with another.

Key terms

Soviets
Councils of workers and soldiers.

Bolsheviks (later known as Communists)
Began in 1903 as a breakaway group from the revolutionary Social Democrat Party (SDs).

Provisional Government
Drawn from the remnants of the Russian parliament which ended in 1917, it attempted to govern Russia between February and October 1917.

February Revolution
The collapse of the tsarist monarchy in February 1917.

Marxists
Believers in the theories of the German revolutionary Karl Marx (1818–83), who taught that history and took the form of a series of violent class struggles.

Proletariat
The revolutionary working class.

Dialectic
The dynamic force that drives history along a predestined path.

USSR
The Union of Soviet Socialist Republics.

Key terms

Red Terror
The brutal methods adopted by Lenin to destroy opposition.

Democratic centralism
The notion that true democracy in the Bolshevik Party lay in the obedience of the members to the instructions of the leaders.

CPSU
The Communist Party of the Soviet Union.

Bourgeoisie
The exploiting capitalists.

Key dates

February Revolution: 1917

October Revolution: 1917

Consolidation of Bolshevik power: 1917–24

Russian Civil War: 1918–20

Foreign interventions: 1918–20

The Red Terror: 1918–20

Key question
What were the main features of the authoritarian system Lenin had established?

Nevertheless, Lenin was careful always to describe his policies as democratic. But for him the term had a particular meaning. Democracy was not to be reckoned as a matter of numbers but as a method of Party rule. Because the Party was the vehicle of historical change, its role was not to win large-scale backing but to direct the Revolution from above, regardless of the scale of popular support. 'No revolution,' Lenin wrote, 'ever waits for formal majorities.' Moreover, since authority flowed from the centre outwards, it was the role of the leaders to lead, the duty of the Party members to follow. The special term describing this was **democratic centralism**. Lenin defined it in these terms:

> Classes are led by parties, and parties are led by individuals who are called leaders. This is the ABC. The will of a class is sometimes fulfilled by a dictator. Soviet socialist democracy is not in the least incompatible with individual rule and dictatorship. What is necessary is individual rule, the recognition of the dictatorial powers of one man. All phrases about equal rights are nonsense.

Lenin asserted unequivocally that the working class was not capable of acting in a revolutionary way unless it was led from above. This was because the workers simply did not know enough. Lenin was unashamedly elitist in this respect. He considered that, left to themselves, the workers would achieve nothing substantial. They would, he said, develop 'only a trade unionist self-consciousness', by which he meant that they would spend their time merely trying to improve their conditions. This being so, it was the task of the informed and enlightened leaders of the **CPSU** who understood history and society to guide and instruct the workers in their true revolutionary role.

> The blind unfolding of the labour movement can lead only to the permeation of that movement with a bourgeois ideology, because the unconscious growth of the labour movement takes the form of trade unionism, and trade unionism signifies the mental enslavement of the workers to the **bourgeoisie**.

Authoritarianism

Lenin's greatest bequest to Soviet Russia was authoritarianism. He returned Russia to the absolutism that it had known under the tsars. In that sense Bolshevism was a continuation of, not a break with, Russia's past. The basic apparatus of Stalin's later oppression was in place at Lenin's death. The main features of Lenin's authoritarian rule between 1917 and 1924 on which Stalin was subsequently to build his own absolute power were:

- The one-party state – all parties other than the Bolsheviks had been outlawed.
- The bureaucratic state – despite the Bolsheviks' original belief in the withering away of the state, central power increased under Lenin and the number of government institutions and officials grew.

- The police state – the Cheka was the first of a series of secret police organisations in Soviet Russia whose task was to impose government control over the people.
- The ban on **factionalism** – introduced by Lenin in 1921, prevented criticism of the leadership within the Party and was, in effect, a ban on free speech.
- The destruction of the trade unions – with Lenin's encouragement, Trotsky (see pages 20–1) had destroyed the independence of the trade unions, with the result that the Russian workers were entirely at the mercy of the state.
- The politicising of the law – under Lenin, the law was not operated as a means of protecting society and the individual but as an extension of political control. He declared that the task of the courts was to apply revolutionary justice. 'The court is not to eliminate terror but to legitimise it.'
- Purges and show trials – the system which was to become a notorious feature of Stalinism (see page 60) had first been created under Lenin. Outstanding examples were the public trials of the Moscow clergy between April and July 1922 and of the **SRs** between June and August of the same year.
- Concentration camps – at the time of Lenin's death there were 315 such camps. Developed as part of the Red Terror they held **White** prisoners of war, rebel peasants and political prisoners, such as SRs, who were considered a threat to Soviet authority.
- Prohibition of public worship – the **Orthodox churches** had been looted then closed, their clergy arrested or dispersed and atheism adopted as a replacement for religious belief.
- The attempt to construct an entirely new society in the USSR.

2 | The Shaping of Soviet Society under Lenin

Stalin was to become notorious for his attempt to create a new type of human being in the Soviet Union, *Homo sovieticus*. But he did not start from scratch. The move towards change had already been instigated by Lenin. It is one of the most significant aspects of Lenin's legacy and worthy of special consideration in this study of the Soviet world that Stalin inherited.

Culture and the arts

After the 1917 Revolution, the Bolsheviks claimed that their triumph had liberated the people from the weaknesses that had tainted all previous societies. The people were now ready to be moulded into a new species. Lenin was reported to have said, 'Man can be made whatever we want him to be.' Trotsky claimed that the aim of the Communist state was 'to produce a new, "improved" version of man'.

The critical aspect of what Lenin and Trotsky believed was that this process would not happen of its own accord. It would have to be directed; people would have to be moulded, culture would have

Key terms

Factionalism
The forming within the Party of groups with a particular complaint or grievance.

SRs
Socialist Revolutionaries, the largest of the revolutionary parties in Russia until outlawed by the Bolsheviks after 1917.

White
Counter-revolutionary.

Orthodox Church
The official state religion of tsarist Russia.

Homo sovieticus
A mock Latin term invented to describe the new 'Soviet man'.

Key dates

Ban on factionalism: 1921

Purges and show trials: 1922

Key terms

Proletkult
Proletarian culture.

**Commissar of
Enlightenment**
Equivalent to an
arts minister.
'Commissar' was a
Soviet term for a
high-ranking official
or officer.

Key figure

**Anatoli
Lunarcharsky
(1875–1933)**
Marxist writer, critic
and playwright
passionately
committed to the
idea of raising the
cultural and
educational
standards of
ordinary Russians.

to be shaped. This further emphasised the dominant role of the
state. The result was that after a brief period of apparent artistic
freedom, culture came under state control. The outstanding
example was the **Proletkult** movement. In theory, this was the
spontaneous creation by the workers of a new Russian culture. In
practice, there was little genuine contribution from ordinary
people. Cultural expression was the preserve of a small artistic
establishment – writers, composers, artists and film makers.

Proletkult predated the Revolution. It had begun earlier in the
century as a movement led by **Anatoli Lunarcharsky** with the aim
and mission of educating the masses. Lenin saw in it a means of
extending Bolshevik control. In 1917 he appointed Lunarcharsky
as **Commissar of Enlightenment**, roughly equivalent to an arts
minister. Lunarcharsky planned to use Proletkult as 'a source of
agitation and propaganda'. The purpose was to attack and destroy
the reactionary prejudices and attitudes of pre-revolutionary
Russia.

It had been Lenin's original hope that after October 1917 the
new revolutionary Russia would see a flowering of culture. The
word culture is not easy to define precisely. In one obvious sense it
refers to the refined aspects of life, such as music, art, sculpture
and writing. But in the sense that Marx and Lenin understood
culture, these things did not exist separately: they were an
expression of the class structure of society itself. That was what
Trotsky meant when he said that 'every ruling class creates its own
culture'. Just as a feudal society has a feudal culture and a
bourgeois society a bourgeois culture, so, too, a proletarian society,
such as Russia now was, must have a proletarian culture.

The works of writers and artists, therefore, would now express
the values of revolutionary Russia. If they did not, then they
would be unacceptable. As with politics and economics, culture
and artistic expression had to serve the state. There was to be no
place for free expression and individualism. Lenin laid it down
that 'the purpose of art and literature is to serve the people'.

There were some Bolsheviks who believed that a new people's
culture would grow naturally out of the existing conditions. Lenin
rejected this. He was not prepared to wait for such an evolution.
The task was to eradicate the remnants of Russia's cultural past
and construct a new, wholly socialist, form. That is why he
approved of Proletkult's willingness to see its role not as narrowly
cultural but as covering all aspects of life including politics and
religion. By 1922, a range of Proletkult artistic and sporting
organisations had been set up across Russia. These included:

- writers' circles
- amateur dramatic groups, including street theatre
- art studios
- poetry workshops
- musical appreciation societies.

Many of these were based in factories. There was even a 'Proletarian University' specially set up in Moscow for factory workers. On the surface, all this seemed to indicate a flowering of workers' culture, but the hard fact was that the art, music, architecture and literature which ordinary people were supposed to enjoy were dictated by the **intelligentsia.** It was they who decided what the workers' tastes should be and who enjoyed such artistic freedom as prevailed after 1917. And even here restrictions soon set in. By 1920, Lenin had become concerned by developments. The artistic control he had originally looked for seemed too loose. He did not want Proletkult to become an independent organisation within the state. He instructed that it be brought under much tighter supervision within Lunarcharsky's Commissariat of Enlightenment. As a result, Proletkult by 1922 had been largely disbanded.

Proletkult's fate was part of the campaign that Lenin launched in 1922 against the intelligentsia, his last major initiative before he died. Angered by criticisms from writers and academics about his policy of War Communism and his New Economic Policy (see page 22), he ordered that strict censorship be imposed on the press and on academic publications. Branded variously as 'counter-revolutionaries, spies and corrupters of student youth', hundreds of writers and university teachers were imprisoned or sent into exile.

It was not a totally dark picture. Literacy in the Soviet Union rose from 43 per cent to 51 per cent of the population. Some of the arts did reach a wider audience and works of artistic merit were produced. Experimentation with form was allowable, hence abstract art was permitted. But the content, the substance, had to be socialist. The meaning or message of a work, whether poem, play, novel, sculpture or opera, had to be pro-government. Anything critical of the Communist system, however well dressed up or packaged, was not tolerated.

This was typified by Lenin himself. As a younger man he had loved classical music, particularly Beethoven's late string quartets which sent him into raptures. But his reaction made him feel ashamed; he was allowing himself to be seduced by a bourgeois notion of beauty. He resolved to give up Beethoven and dedicate himself single-mindedly to revolutionary study.

Religion

Karl Marx had described religion as 'the opium of the people'. He was not being merely dismissive; he was making a profound historical point. His argument was that religious belief and worship were what people turned to in order to deaden the pain of life. Since all periods of history were times of conflict, suffering was ever-present. Only with the victory of the proletariat would people understand there was no longer any need to believe in God and the afterlife. They would then realise that religion was a superstition, used by class oppressors to keep the people down.

Having come to power, Lenin put this Marxist notion into action. Revolutionary Russia with the proletariat now in control was to be a secular state with no place for organised religion. This intention was

Intelligentsia
The group in society distinguished by their intellectual or creative abilities, e.g. writers, artists, composers, teachers.

Key term

Key question
Why were the Bolsheviks so determined to destroy religious faith?

Key date

Decree on Separation
of Church and State:
20 January 1918

immediately declared in the Decree on Separation of Church and
State. This measure had two aims: to break the hold of the clergy
and to undermine the religious faith of the peasants, for whom the
Bolsheviks had a particular distaste as representing the most
backward features of old Russia. The main terms of the decree were:

- Church properties were no longer to be owned by the clergy, but
  by the local soviets from whom churches would have to be
  rented for public worship.
- Clergy were no longer to be paid salaries or pensions by the state.
- The Church was no longer to have a central organisation with
  authority over local congregations.
- Religious teaching was forbidden in schools.

Over the next three years the Bolsheviks used this decree to wage
war against the Orthodox Church. Its leaders, such as
Metropolitan (Archbishop) Benjamin, its chief spokesman in
Moscow who dared to speak out against the regime and its
methods, were subjected to a show trial before being imprisoned.
By the time of Lenin's death in 1924, over 300 bishops had been
executed and some 10,000 priests imprisoned or exiled. The head
of the Church, Patriarch Tikhon, at first resisted bravely, issuing
powerful denunciations of the godless attacks upon the Church,
but he then broke under the stress and became subservient to the
regime, which used him thereafter as a puppet.

It soon became common practice for churches and monasteries
to be looted and desecrated by the *Cheka* acting under government
direction. Such moves were backed by a widespread propaganda
campaign to ridicule religion and the Church. The press poured
out daily mockeries. Plays and street theatre presentations
sometimes subtly, more often crudely, jeered at the absurdities of
faith and worship. Judaism and Islam did not escape: these faiths,
too, were pilloried.

Religion was too deeply embedded in Russian tradition for it to
be totally eradicated in this way, but it was driven underground.
Peasants continued to pray and worship as their forebears had, but
they could no longer risk doing so publicly.

Key term

Capitalism
The predominant
economic system in
Europe and the
USA, based on
private ownership
and the making of
profits –
condemned by
Marxists as involving
the exploitation of
the poor by the rich.

Women and the family

It was a firm Marxist belief that women were abused under
capitalism. The principal instrument of their subjection was
marriage. This one-sided social contract turned women into victims
since it made them, in effect, the property of their husbands. It was
the perfect example of the exploitative capitalist system. It was not
surprising, therefore, that on taking power the Bolsheviks should
have taken immediate steps to raise the status of women and
undermine marriage as an institution. In the two years after 1917,
decrees had been introduced which included such innovations as:

Key question
How did the status of
women change in
Bolshevik Russia?

- legal divorce if either partner requested it
- recognition of illegitimate children as full citizens
- legalising of abortion
- the state to be responsible for the raising of children.

These changes derived from the notion that 'love' was a bourgeois concept based on a false view of the relations between the sexes and between parents and children. It was believed that, once such romantic nonsense was recognised for what it was, a structured, ordered society would follow. However, plans for setting up large boarding schools where children would be permanently removed from their parents and brought up in social equality were soon dropped. It was simply too costly. There were also growing doubts about whether the attack on the family was well advised.

It is always easier to be revolutionary in political matters than in social ones. The family was the traditional social unit in Russia and it proved impossible to replace it simply on the basis of a theory. Where would the carers of the young come from? Were there not biological and emotional bonds between parents and children with which it would be dangerous to tamper? It was an area where Marxism–Leninism did not have any workable answers. It is significant that in a later period Stalin strongly disapproved of divorce and insisted on the social value of the family as the basic unit in Soviet society (see page 122).

Alexandra Kollontai

The outstanding woman in the party was Alexandra Kollontai (1872–1952). She was the voice of early Russian feminism and a pioneer among Bolshevik women. In her writings she advanced the idea that women need to be liberated sexually, politically and psychologically. She argued that free love was the only relationship that guaranteed equality for women. For her, the family was a prison; children should be reared by society at large.

Kollontai was a fascinating woman and an important international feminist, but she was untypical as a Bolshevik. It might be thought that, given the views of Kollontai and the general desire of the Bolsheviks to eradicate old values, revolutionary Russia would become a hotbed of sexual licence. It did not quite work that way. The Bolsheviks were an odd mixture of permissiveness and puritanism. Lenin was unimpressed by Kollontai's feminism. He found her emphasis on free love and casual relationships unwelcome in a society which under his direction was aiming at socialist conformity.

3 | Lenin's Legacy
The absolute right of the CPSU to rule

The belief of Lenin and the Bolsheviks that they were the special agents of historical change led logically to their destruction of all other political parties. Since history was on their side, the Bolsheviks had the right to absolute control. Initially, there were protests from within the Bolshevik Party over this. Some members, who had hoped that Bolshevik rule would be both socialist and democratic, were disturbed by Lenin's assumption that he was entitled to direct the lives of the ordinary people of Russia. **Maxim Gorky** warned:

Key question
What legacy did Lenin leave the USSR?

Maxim Gorky (1868–1936)
Novelist and playwright, arguably the most influential of all Soviet writers.

Key figure

Key figures

Lev Kamenev (1883–1936)
A leading Bolshevik, he held various key official positions under Lenin between 1917 and 1924.

Grigory Zinoviev (1883–1936)
A close colleague of Lenin since the formation of the Bolshevik Party in 1903, he played a key role in the October Revolution and became Chairman of the Comintern.

Lenin is a gifted man who has all the qualities of a leader, including these essential ones: lack of morality and a merciless, lordly harshness towards the lives of the masses. As long as I can, I will repeat to the Russian proletariat, 'You are being led to destruction, you are being used as material in an inhuman experiment; to your leaders, you are not human.'

Gorky's warning raises the question which historians continue to discuss: whether the brutal totalitarianism of the Stalinist regime which operated from the late 1920s (see page 60) was the responsibility solely of Stalin, or whether it was a logical development of the system previously established under Lenin. What can now be said is that the 6724 letters in Lenin's private correspondence, which became available for scrutiny in the 1990s, reveal that the brutal methods which Lenin adopted after 1917 caused him no qualms. In reviewing Robert Service's biography, Dominic Lieven concludes that Lenin was motivated by hatred. He writes of:

Lenin's huge visceral hatred for old Russia: for the Romanovs of course above all and for the old upper and middle classes, but also for the whole of old Russian culture … In no circumstances would 20th-century Russian history have been pleasant or bloodless. But Lenin made it far worse than it needed to be. In 1917 he combined fanaticism, ruthlessness and absolute self-confidence with a terrifying naivety about government, economics and Russian society. To impose such immense sacrifices in the name of so naive and flawed a vision makes Lenin one of the greatest criminals of the 20th century.

Lenin's succession

Key question
What plans had Lenin made for his succession?

Key dates

Lenin's Testament: 1923

Death of Lenin: 21 January 1924

Between 1922 and 1924 Lenin suffered a series of strokes which left him partially paralysed and unable to speak. Because he was so unwell during what proved to be the last two years of his life he had no opportunity to prepare for his succession. He gave no clear indication as to the type of government that should follow him. There were suggestions that he favoured some form of collective leadership, but this cannot be known for sure since he left no precise instructions. What he did leave were a set of comments on the character of his leading Bolshevik colleagues. These notes which date from January 1923 and which became known as 'Lenin's Testament' were highly critical. On the basis of what he said, there was no outstanding colleague worthy of taking up the reins of leadership. He was especially severe on Joseph Stalin (see page 13).

The problem was that Lenin not only failed to name a replacement, he effectively prevented any other choice being made by pointing out the weaknesses in all the other likely candidates, Trotsky, **Kamenev**, **Zinoviev** and **Bukharin**. The result was that at Lenin's death in January 1924, the 'Testament' had still not been made public. With hindsight, we can see that this made a power struggle after his death unavoidable.

In his last writings in 1923 Lenin, doubtless aware of the problem he was leaving the Party, warned the comrades against

Key figure

Nicolai Bukharin (1888–1938)
The leading economic thinker in the Party, he had helped organise the Bolshevik takeover in Moscow in 1917.

allowing the Party and government to lose their revolutionary character by becoming mired in routine and bureaucracy. 'Our state apparatus is so deplorable, so wretched,' he wrote. The irony was that he, more than anyone, was responsible for the growth of the bureaucracy which he now condemned.

The international issue

A critical aspect of Lenin's impact on Russia relates to the place of the USSR in the world. As an international revolutionary, Lenin had originally expected that the successful Bolshevik seizure of power in October 1917 would be the first stage in a worldwide proletarian uprising. When this proved mistaken, he had to adjust to a situation in which Bolshevik Russia became an isolated revolutionary state, beset by internal and external enemies. This involved him in another major modification of Marxist theory. Marx had taught that proletarian revolution would be an international class movement. Yet the 1917 Revolution had been the work not of a class but of a party and had been restricted to one nation.

Lenin explained this in terms of a delayed revolution: the international rising would occur at some point in the future; in the interim, Soviet Russia must consolidate its own individual revolution. This placed the Bolshevik government and its international agency, the **Comintern**, in an ambiguous position. What was their essential role to be? At Lenin's death, this question – whether the USSR's primary aim was world revolution or national survival – was still unresolved. It would be Stalin's task to attempt to provide an answer.

Key question
What problem did Lenin leave the USSR on the international front?

Comintern
Set up in 1919 to organise world revolution.

Key term

Summary diagram: Lenin's Russia, 1917–24

Ban on criticism and free speech

Destruction of the trade unions

The secret police

Concentration camps

Lenin's legacy

Purges and show trials introduced

USSR's international role left unresolved

Restriction on religious freedom

The one-party, bureaucratic state

Uncertain succession to the leadership of Soviet Russia

2 Stalin's Rise to Power

POINTS TO CONSIDER

When Lenin, the Bolshevik leader, died he left many problems but no obvious successor. Few Russian Communists gave thought to Stalin as a likely leader. Yet five years later, after a bitter power struggle, it was Stalin who had outmanoeuvred his rivals and established his authority over the Party and the nation. How he achieved this is the subject of this chapter whose main themes are:

- Lenin and Stalin
- The power struggle after Lenin's death
- The defeat of Trotsky and the Left
- The defeat of the Right.

Key dates

1924	Death of Lenin
	Politburo declared USSR to be ruled by collective leadership
	Lenin's Testament suppressed
1925	Trotsky lost his position as War Commissar
	Kamenev and Zinoviev headed 'United Opposition'
1926	Trotsky joined Kamenev and Zinoviev in Left political bloc, defeated by Stalin's supporters
1927	Stalin persuaded Congress to expel Trotsky from CPSU
1928	Stalin attacked Right over agricultural policy
1929	Leading figures on Right finally defeated by Stalin and demoted in CPSU
	Trotsky exiled from USSR

1 | Lenin and Stalin

Most historians used to believe that Stalin's pre-1924 career was unimportant. They accepted the description of him by **Nicolai Sukhanov**, dating from 1922, as a 'dull, grey blank'. But researches in the Soviet archives over the past 20 years have indicated that the notion of Stalin as a nonentity is the opposite of the truth. A leading British authority, Robert Service, has shown that Stalin was very highly regarded by Lenin and played a central role in the Bolshevik Party. Another British scholar, Simon Sebag Montefiore, in an exhaustive study of Stalin's early career, has stressed that Stalin was an indispensable Bolshevik organiser before 1917. He was the brains behind so many of the violent campaigns that raised money for the Party.

Before 1917 the Bolshevik Party had been only a few thousand strong and Lenin had known the great majority of members personally. He had been impressed by Stalin's organising ability, insensitivity to suffering, and willingness to obey orders. He once described him as 'that wonderful **Georgian**', a reference to his work as an agitator among the non-Russian peoples. With Lenin's backing, Stalin had risen by 1912 to become one of the six members of the Central Committee, the policy-making body of the Bolshevik Party. He had also helped to found the Party's newspaper, *Pravda*.

The October Revolution and Civil War

Having spent the war years, 1914–17, in exile in Siberia, Stalin returned to Petrograd in March 1917. His role in the October Revolution is difficult to disentangle. Official accounts, written after he had taken power, were a mixture of distortion and invention, with any unflattering episodes omitted. What is reasonably certain is that Stalin was loyal to Lenin after the latter's return to Petrograd in April 1917. Lenin instructed the Bolsheviks to abandon all co-operation with other parties and to devote themselves to preparing for a seizure of power. As a Leninist, Stalin was opposed to the **'October deserters'**, such as Kamenev and Zinoviev.

During the period of crisis and civil war that accompanied the efforts of the Bolsheviks to consolidate their authority after 1917, Stalin's non-Russian background proved invaluable. His knowledge of the minority peoples of the old Russian Empire led to his being appointed **Commissar for Nationalities**. Lenin had believed that Stalin's toughness well qualified him for this role. As Commissar, Stalin became the ruthless Bolshevik organiser for the whole of the Caucasus region during the Civil War from 1918 to 1920. This led to a number of disputes with Trotsky, the Bolshevik Commissar for War. Superficially the quarrels were about strategy and tactics, but at a deeper level they were a clash of wills. They proved to be the beginning of a deep personal rivalry between Stalin and Trotsky.

Sources of dispute

Although Stalin had been completely loyal to Lenin, there were two particular occasions when he had aroused Lenin's anger. After the Civil War had ended, Stalin, despite being himself a Georgian, had been curt and off-hand in discussions with the representatives from Georgia. Lenin, anxious to gain the support of the national minorities for the Bolshevik regime, had to intervene personally to prevent the Georgians leaving in a huff. On another occasion, in a more directly personal matter, Lenin learned from his wife, Krupskaya, that in a row over the Georgian question Stalin had subjected her to 'a storm of the coarsest abuse', telling her to keep her nose out of state affairs, and calling her 'a whore'. The very day that Lenin was informed of this, 22 December 1922, he dictated his 'Testament' as a direct response.

His main criticism read: 'Comrade Stalin, since becoming General Secretary of the Party in 1922, has concentrated enormous power in his hands; and I am not sure he always knows how to exercise that power with sufficient caution.' In a later postscript, Lenin again stressed Stalin's rudeness, which was unacceptable in a General Secretary who should be a person of tact capable of preventing divisions developing within the Party. Lenin went on to urge the comrades 'to think about ways of removing Comrade Stalin from that position'. But this was not done. Lenin was too ill during the last year of his life to be politically active. At his death in January 1924, he had still not taken any formal steps to remove Stalin, and the Testament had not been made public.

Profile: Joseph Stalin (1879–1953) (career to 1924)

1879	– Born in Georgia
1899	– His revolutionary activities led to expulsion from Tiflis seminary
1905	– Met Lenin for first time
1907	– Organised the Tiflis atrocity
1912	– Adopted the name Stalin
	– Became a member of the Central Committee of the Bolshevik Party
	– Helped to found *Pravda*, the Bolshevik newspaper
1914–17	– In exile in Siberia
1917	– Returned to Petrograd
	– Became People's Commissar for Nationalities
1919	– Liaison Officer between Politburo and Orgburo
	– Head of the Workers' and Peasants' Inspectorate
1922	– General Secretary of the Communist (Bolshevik) Party
1924	– Delivered the oration at Lenin's funeral

Stalin, meaning 'man of steel', was not his real name. It was simply the name he adopted in 1912, the last in a series of 10 aliases that Joseph Vissarionovich Djugashvili had used to avoid detection as a revolutionary.

A bloody heritage

He was born in Georgia, a rugged province in the south of the Russian Empire, renowned for the fierceness of its people. Blood feuds and family vendettas were common. Georgia had only recently been incorporated into the Russian Empire. Tsarist government officials often wrote in exasperation of the difficulties of trying to control a savage people who refused to accept their subordination to Russia.

Seminary studies

Such was the stock from which Stalin came. His drunken father eked out a miserable existence as a cobbler and the family appears to have lived in constant poverty. There have been suggestions that both Stalin's admiration of all things Russian and his contempt for middle-class intellectuals derived from a sense of resentment over his humble non-Russian origins. Stalin's mother was a particularly devout woman and it was largely through her influence that her son was enrolled as a student in a Georgian-Orthodox seminary in Tiflis, the capital of Georgia. This did not denote religious fervour on Stalin's part. The fact was that at this time in imperial Russia attendance at a church academy was the only way to obtain a Russian-style education, an essential requirement for anyone from the provinces who had ambition. Stalin seems to have been attracted less by theology than by the political ideas with which he came into contact.

The young activist

In the seminary records for 1899 there is an entry beside Stalin's name that reads 'Expelled for not attending lessons – reasons unknown.' We now know the reasons: he had become involved in the Georgian resistance movement, agitating against tsarist control. His anti-government activities drew him into the Social Democratic Workers' Party. From the time of his expulsion from the seminary to the Revolution of 1917 Stalin was a committed follower of Lenin. He threw himself into the task of raising funds for the Bolsheviks; his specialities were bank hold-ups and train robberies.

Violent crime

His most notorious success occurred in 1907 when he plotted the seizure of a wagon train delivering notes and bullion to the largest bank in Tiflis. In a scene reminiscent of the American Wild West, police and guards were mown down in a hail of rifle and pistol fire; bombs were then thrown under the wagons, blowing men and horses into bloody fragments and shattering the windows of the buildings that overlooked Yerevan Square where the bank stood. Notes, bullion and bank boxes were grabbed and bundled into waiting horse carriages which were then frantically driven off in great clouds of dust while onlookers cowered in fear of their lives. Fifty people died in the raid and as many were seriously injured. The Bolshevik raiders made off with the equivalent of £1.7 million.

Imprisonment

By 1917 Stalin had been arrested eight times and had been sentenced to various periods of imprisonment and exile. Afterwards he tended to despise those revolutionaries who had escaped such experiences by fleeing to the relative comfort of self-imposed exile abroad.

Key question
How had Stalin been able to rise up the Bolshevik ranks?

Key terms

Council of People's Commissars
A cabinet of ministers, responsible for creating government policies.

Secretariat
A form of civil service, responsible for carrying out those policies.

Orgburo
The Workers' and Peasants' Inspectorate.

Patronage
The right to appoint individuals to official posts in the Party and government.

Stalin's position in 1924

In the uncertain atmosphere that followed Lenin's death, a number of pieces of luck helped Stalin promote his own claims. However, it would be wrong to ascribe his success wholly to good fortune. Stalin may have lacked brilliance, but he had great ability. His particular qualities of perseverance and willingness to undertake laborious administrative work were ideally suited to the times.

The government of Soviet Russia, as it had developed by 1924, had two main features: the **Council of People's Commissars** and the **Secretariat**. Both these bodies were staffed and controlled by the Bolshevik Party. It has to be stressed that the vital characteristic of this governmental system was that the Party ruled. By 1922 Soviet Russia was a one-party state. Membership of that one party was essential for all who held government posts at whatever level.

As government grew in scope, certain posts, which initially had not been considered especially significant, began to provide their holders with the levers of power. This had not been the intention, but was the unforeseen result of the emerging pattern of Bolshevik rule. It was in this context that Stalin's previous appointments to key posts in both government and Party proved vital. These had been:

- **People's Commissar for Nationalities (1917)** In this post, Stalin was in charge of the officials in the many regions and republics that made up the USSR (the official title of the Soviet state after 1922). *Head Central control*
- **Liaison Officer between Politburo and Orgburo (1919)** This post placed him in a unique position to monitor both the Party's policy and the Party's personnel.
- **Head of the Workers' and Peasants' Inspectorate (1919)** This position entitled him to oversee the work of all government departments.
- **General Secretary of the Communist Party (1922)** In this position, he recorded and conveyed Party policy. This enabled him to build up personal files on all the members of the Party. Nothing of note happened that Stalin did not know about.

Stalin became the indispensable link in the chain of command in the Communist Party and the Soviet government. Above all, what these posts gave him was the power of **patronage**. He used this authority to place his own supporters in key positions. Since they then owed their place to him, Stalin could count on their support in the voting in the various committees which made up the organisation of the Party and the government.

Such were the levers in Stalin's possession during the Party in-fighting over the succession to Lenin. No other contender came anywhere near matching Stalin in his hold on the Party machine. Whatever the ability of the individuals or groups who opposed him, he could always out-vote and out-manoeuvre them.

The Lenin enrolment

Stalin had also gained advantage from recent changes in the structure of the Communist Party. Between 1923 and 1925 the Party had set out to increase the number of true proletarians in its ranks. This was known as 'the Lenin enrolment'. It resulted in the membership of the CPSU rising from 340,000 in 1922 to 600,000 by 1925.

The new members were predominantly poorly educated and politically unsophisticated, but they were fully aware that the many privileges which came with Party membership depended on their being loyal to those who had first invited them into the Bolshevik ranks. The task of vetting the Lenin enrolment had fallen largely to the officials in the Secretariat who worked directly under Stalin as General Secretary. In this way, the expansion of the Party added to his growing power of patronage. It provided him with a reliable body of votes in the various Party committees at local and central level.

Key question
What was the significance for Stalin of 'the Lenin enrolment'?

The attack upon factionalism

Another lasting feature of Lenin's period in power that proved of great value to Stalin was what had become known as the 'attack upon factionalism'. This referred to Lenin's condemnation in 1921 of divisions within the Party (see page 4). What this rejection of 'factionalism' effectively did was to frustrate any serious attempt to criticise Party decisions or policies. It became extremely difficult to mount any form of legitimate opposition within the CPSU. Stalin benefited directly from the ban on criticism of the Party line. The charge of factionalism provided him with a ready weapon for resisting challenges to the authority he had begun to exercise.

Key question
How did Lenin's 'attack upon factionalism' help Stalin?

The Lenin legacy

There was an accompanying factor that legitimised Stalin's position. Stalin became heir to the 'Lenin legacy'. By this is meant the tradition of authority and leadership that Lenin had established during his lifetime, and the veneration in which he was held after his death. It is barely an exaggeration to say that in the eyes of the Communist Party, Lenin became a god. His actions and decisions became unchallengeable, and all arguments and disputes within the Party were settled by reference to his statements and writings. Lenin became the measure of the correctness of Soviet theory and practice. Soviet Communism became Leninism. After 1924, if a Party member could assume the mantle of Lenin and appear to carry on Lenin's work, he would establish a formidable claim to power. This is exactly what Stalin began to do.

Key question
How did the 'Lenin legacy' benefit Stalin?

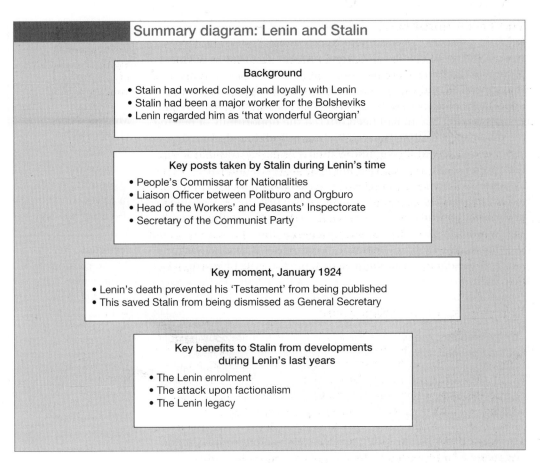

Summary diagram: Lenin and Stalin

Background
- Stalin had worked closely and loyally with Lenin
- Stalin had been a major worker for the Bolsheviks
- Lenin regarded him as 'that wonderful Georgian'

Key posts taken by Stalin during Lenin's time
- People's Commissar for Nationalities
- Liaison Officer between Politburo and Orgburo
- Head of the Workers' and Peasants' Inspectorate
- Secretary of the Communist Party

Key moment, January 1924
- Lenin's death prevented his 'Testament' from being published
- This saved Stalin from being dismissed as General Secretary

Key benefits to Stalin from developments during Lenin's last years
- The Lenin enrolment
- The attack upon factionalism
- The Lenin legacy

2 | The Power Struggle after Lenin's Death

Lenin's funeral

Immediately after Lenin's death, the **Politburo**, whose members were Stalin, Trotsky, **Rykov**, **Tomsky**, Kamenev and Zinoviev, publicly proclaimed their intention to continue as a collective leadership, but behind the scenes the competition for individual authority had already begun. In the manoeuvring, Stalin gained an advantage by being the one to deliver the oration at Lenin's funeral. The sight of Stalin as leading mourner suggested a continuity between him and Lenin, an impression heightened by the contents of his speech in which, in the name of the Party, he humbly dedicated himself to follow in the tradition of the departed leader:

> In leaving us, Comrade Lenin commanded us to keep the unity of our Party. We swear to thee, Comrade Lenin, to honour thy command. In leaving us, Comrade Lenin ordered us to maintain and strengthen the dictatorship of the proletariat. We swear to thee, Comrade Lenin, to exert our full strength in honouring thy command.

Key question
What were Stalin's advantages in his leadership struggle with Trotsky?

Key term

Politburo
The inner cabinet of the ruling Central Committee of the CPSU.

Key dates

Death of Lenin: 1924

Politburo declared USSR to be ruled by collective leadership: 1924

Since Stalin's speech was the first crucial move to promote himself as Lenin's successor, it was to be expected that Trotsky, his chief rival, would try to counter it in some way. Yet Trotsky was not even present at the funeral. It was a very conspicuous absence, and it is still difficult to understand why Trotsky did not appreciate the importance of appearances following Lenin's death in January 1924. Initially he, not Stalin, had been offered the opportunity of making the major speech at the funeral. But not only did he decline this, he also failed to attend the ceremony itself. His excuse was that Stalin had given him the wrong date, but this simply was not true. Documents show that he learned the real date early enough for him to have reached Moscow with time to spare. Instead he continued his planned journey and was on holiday on the day of the funeral. This was hardly the image of a dedicated Leninist.

What makes Trotsky's behaviour even odder is that he was well aware of the danger that Stalin represented. In 1924 he prophesied that Stalin would become 'the dictator of the USSR'. He also gave a remarkable analysis of the basis of Stalin's power in the Party:

> He is needed by all of them; by the tired radicals, by the bureaucrats, by the **Nepmen**, the upstarts, by all the worms that are crawling out of the upturned soil of the manured revolution. He knows how to meet them on their own ground, he speaks their language and he knows how to lead them. He has the deserved reputation of an old revolutionary. He has will and daring. Right now he is organising around himself the sneaks of the Party, the artful dodgers.

This was a bitter but strikingly accurate assessment of how Stalin had made a large part of the Party dependent on him. But logically such awareness on Trotsky's part should have made him eager to prevent Stalin from stealing the advantage. His reluctance to act is a fascinating feature of Trotsky's puzzling character.

Trotsky's character

Trotsky had a complex personality. He was one of those figures in history who may be described as having been their own worst enemy. Despite his many gifts and intellectual brilliance, he had serious weaknesses that undermined his chances of success. At times, he was unreasonably self-assured; at other critical times, he suffered from diffidence and lack of judgement. An example of this had occurred earlier, at the time of Stalin's mishandling of the Georgian question. Lenin's anger with Stalin had offered Trotsky a golden opportunity for undermining Stalin's position, but for some reason Trotsky had declined to attack.

A possible clue to his reluctance is that he felt inhibited by his Jewishness. Trotsky knew that, in a nation such as Russia with its deeply ingrained **anti-Semitism**, his race made him an outsider. A remarkable example of his awareness of this occurred in 1917, when Lenin offered him the post of Deputy Chairman of the Soviet government. Trotsky rejected it on the grounds that his appointment would be an embarrassment to Lenin and the government. 'It would,' he said, 'give enemies grounds for

Key figures

Aleksei Rykov (1881–1938) Chairman of the Central Committee of the CPSU.

Mikhail Tomsky (1880–1937) The minister responsible for representing (in practice controlling) the trade unions.

Key terms

Nepmen Those farmers and traders who were considered to have unfairly exploited the New Economic Policy, introduced by Lenin in 1921, to line their own pockets.

Anti-Semitism Hatred of the Jewish race – for centuries Russia had been notorious for its virulent treatment of the Jews.

Key question What were Trotsky's weaknesses?

claiming that the country was ruled by a Jew.' It may have been similar reasoning that allowed Stalin to gain an advantage over him at the time of Lenin's funeral.

Suppression of Lenin's Testament

A dangerous hurdle in Stalin's way was Lenin's Testament (see page 13). If it were to be published, Stalin would be gravely damaged by its contents. However, here, as so often during this period, fortune favoured him. Had the document been made public, not only would Lenin's criticisms of Stalin have been revealed, but also those concerning Trotsky, Zinoviev and Kamenev. Nearly all the members of the Politburo had reason for suppressing the Testament.

When the members of the Central Committee were presented with the document in May 1924, they realised that it was too damning broadly to be used exclusively against any one individual. They agreed to its being shelved indefinitely. Trotsky, for obvious personal reasons, went along with the decision, but in doing so he was declining yet another opportunity to challenge Stalin's right to power. In fact it was Trotsky, not Stalin, whom the Politburo regarded as the greater danger.

Attitudes towards Trotsky

Kamenev and Zinoviev joined Stalin in an unofficial **triumvirate** within the Politburo. Their aim was to isolate Trotsky by exploiting his unpopularity with large sections of the Party. The 'Lenin enrolment' helped them in this. The new proletarian members were hardly the type of men to be impressed by the cultured Trotsky. The seemingly down-to-earth Stalin was much more to their liking.

The attitude of Party members towards Trotsky was an important factor in the weakening of his position. Colleagues tended to regard Trotsky as dangerously ambitious and his rival Stalin as reliably self-effacing. This was because Trotsky was flamboyant and brilliant, while his rival was unspectacular and methodical. Trotsky was the type of person who attracted either admiration or distaste, but seldom loyalty. That was why he lacked a genuine following. It is true that he was highly regarded by the **Red Army**, whose creator he had been, but this was never matched by any comparable political support. Trotsky failed to build a power base within the Party. This invariably gave him the appearance of an outsider.

Adding to his difficulties in this regard was the doubt about his commitment to Bolshevism. Until 1917, as Lenin had noted in his Testament, Trotsky had belonged to the **Mensheviks**. This led to the suspicion that his conversion had been a matter of expediency rather than conviction. Many of the old-guard Bolsheviks regarded Trotsky as a Menshevik turncoat who could not be trusted.

Key date

Lenin's Testament suppressed: May 1924

Key terms

Triumvirate
A ruling or influential bloc of three persons.

Red Army
Between 1918 and 1920, Trotsky, as War Commissar, turned a ramshackle assortment of veterans and untrained recruits into a formidable three million-strong force to defend the Revolution.

Mensheviks
A Marxist party that had split from the Bolsheviks when the SD Party broke up in 1903.

Bureaucratisation

Despite the attacks upon him, Trotsky attempted to fight back. The issue he chose was bureaucratisation. He defined this as the abandonment of genuine discussion within the Party and the growth in power of the Secretariat, which was able to make decisions and operate policies without reference to ordinary Party members.

Trotsky had good reason to think he had chosen a powerful cause. After all, Lenin himself in his last writings had warned the Party against the creeping dangers of bureaucracy. Accordingly, Trotsky pressed his views in the Party Congresses and in the meetings of the Central Committee and the Politburo. His condemnation of the growth of bureaucracy was coupled with an appeal for a return to **'Party democracy'**. He expanded his arguments in a series of essays, the most controversial of which was *Lessons of October*, in which he criticised Kamenev and Zinoviev for their past disagreements with Lenin. The assault was ill judged, since it invited retaliation in kind. Trotsky's Menshevik past and his divergence from Leninism were highlighted in a number of books and pamphlets, most notably Kamenev's *Lenin or Trotsky?*

As a move in the power struggle, Trotsky's campaign for greater Party democracy was misjudged. His censures on bureaucracy left Stalin largely unscathed. In trying to expose the growing bureaucracy in the Communist Party, Trotsky overlooked the essential fact that Bolshevik rule since 1917 had always been bureaucratic. Indeed, it was because the Soviet state functioned as a bureaucracy that Party members received privileges in political and public life. Trotsky's line was hardly likely to gain significant support from Party members who had a vested interest in maintaining the Party's bureaucratic ways.

Key question
What did Trotsky mean by 'bureaucratisation'?

'Party democracy'
Trotsky was not pressing for democracy in the full sense of all Party members having a say. His aim was to condemn the centralising of power from which Stalin had gained such benefit.

Key term

Profile: Lev Trotsky (1879–1940)

1879	– Born into a Ukrainian Jewish family
1898	– Convicted of revolutionary activities and exiled to Siberia
1902	– Adopted the name Trotsky
	– Escaped from exile and joined Lenin in London
1903	– Sided with the Mensheviks in the SD split
1905	– Became Chairman of St Petersburg Soviet
1906	– Exiled again to Siberia
1907	– Escaped again and fled abroad
1907–17	– Lived in various European countries and in USA
1917	– Returned to Petrograd after February Revolution
	– Principal organiser of the October coup
	– Appointed Foreign Affairs Commissar
1918	– Negotiated the Treaty of Brest-Litovsk which formally ended the war with Germany
1918–20	– As War Commissar, created the Red Army
1921	– Suppressed the Kronstadt Rising
	– Destroyed the trade unions in Russia
1924–27	– Outmanoeuvred in the power struggle with Stalin

1927   – Sentenced to internal exile at Alma Ata
1929   – Banished from USSR
1929–40 – Lived in various countries
         – Wrote prodigiously on revolutionary theory, in
           opposition to Stalin
1940   – Assassinated in Mexico on Stalin's orders

Early career

Trotsky's real name was Leon (Lev) Bronstein. He was born into a Jewish landowning family in the Ukraine in 1879. Rebellious from an early age, he sided with the peasants on his family's estate. Yet, like Lenin, he rejected '**economism**', the attempt to raise the standards of peasants and workers by improving their conditions. He wanted to intensify class warfare by exploiting grievances, not to lessen it by introducing reforms.

As a revolutionary, Trotsky's sympathies lay with the Mensheviks and it was as a Menshevik that he became president of the St Petersburg Soviet during the 1905 Revolution. His activities led to his arrest and exile. Between 1907 and 1917 he lived in a variety of foreign countries, developing his theory of 'permanent revolution'.

Following the collapse of tsardom in the February Revolution, Trotsky returned to Petrograd and immediately joined the Bolshevik Party. He became chairman of the Petrograd Soviet, a position which he used to organise the Bolshevik rising which overthrew the Provisional Government in October 1917.

Commissar for Foreign Affairs

In the Bolshevik government that then took over, Trotsky became Commissar for Foreign Affairs. He was the chief negotiator in the Russo-German talks that resulted in Russia's withdrawal from the war in 1918 under the Treaty of Brest-Litovsk.

Commissar for War

He then became Commissar for War, and achieved what was arguably the greatest success of his career, the victory of the Red Army in the Civil War of 1918–20. As a hardliner, Trotsky fully supported Lenin's repressive policy of War Communism. He plotted the destruction of the Russian trade unions, and in 1921 ordered the suppression of the rebellious Kronstadt workers.

Exile

Trotsky was never fully accepted by his fellow Bolsheviks, which enabled Stalin to isolate him after 1924. In 1929 Trotsky was exiled from the USSR. He spent his last 11 years in a variety of countries. In 1939 he founded the Fourth International, a movement of anti-Stalin Marxists drawn from some 30 countries. Trotsky's end came in 1940 in Mexico City, when a Soviet agent, acting on Stalin's direct orders, killed him by driving an ice-pick into his head.

Key term

Economism
Putting the improvement of the workers' conditions before the need for revolution.

Disputes over the New Economic Policy (NEP)

Trotsky's reputation was further damaged by the issue of the New Economic Policy. NEP has to be understood in relation to the economic problems which the Bolsheviks had had to face between 1917 and 1924. Soon after taking power Lenin had implemented a policy known as 'War Communism'. This was a series of harshly restrictive economic measures which were intended to help the Bolsheviks win the Civil War of 1918–20.

Key question
How was Trotsky weakened by the NEP issue?

- Agriculture and industry were brought under central control.
- Food was seized from the peasants by armed and violent government requisition squads.
- Money was abolished.
- Farming for profit was forbidden.
- Traditional village and town markets for the buying and exchange of goods were forbidden to be held.

Lenin hoped that by such measures the desperate situation created by the Civil War, in particular the famine which had overtaken many Russian provinces, would be eased. Lenin had also judged that a fiercely applied policy of centralisation would help break the resistance of the Whites. However, War Communism did not produce the expected results. The interference with the peasants' traditional ways caused disruption and resentment. Hunger did not lessen: it intensified. Despite the government's terror tactics there were many instances of serious resistance from those who had previously been Bolshevik supporters, the most troubling of these being the **Kronstadt rising** in 1921. Whatever the purity of the revolutionary theory behind War Communism, it had clearly failed to deliver the goods. The peasants had not been coerced into producing larger grain stocks.

Always **pragmatic** in his approach, Lenin decided on a U-turn. He judged that, if the peasants could not be forced, they must be persuaded. The stick had not worked, so now was the time for the carrot. At a Party Congress in 1921 he told members that it made no sense for Bolsheviks to pretend that they could pursue an economic policy which took no account of the real situation. He then announced that War Communism was to be replaced with a New Economic Policy, the main features of which were:

- central economic control to be relaxed
- the requisitioning of grain to be abandoned and replaced by a **tax in kind**
- the peasants to be allowed to keep their food surpluses and sell them for a profit
- public markets to be restored
- money to be reintroduced as a means of trading.

Despite the deep disagreements that were soon to emerge among the Bolsheviks over NEP, the grim economic situation in Russia led the delegates to give unanimous support to Lenin's proposals when they were first introduced.

Key terms

Kronstadt rising
A protest in 1921 by previously loyal workers and sailors at the Kronstadt naval base near Petrograd against the tyranny of Bolshevik rule – the rising was brutally suppressed by the Red Army acting under Trotsky's orders.

Pragmatic
Deciding policy on the basis of fact and circumstance rather than theory.

Tax in kind
The surrendering by the peasant of a certain amount of his produce, equivalent to a fixed sum of money.

Lenin was aware that NEP marked a retreat from the principle of state control of the economy. It restored a mixed economy in which certain features of capitalism existed alongside socialism. Knowing how uneasy this made many Bolsheviks, Lenin stressed that NEP was only a temporary concession to capitalism and that the Party still had control of 'the commanding heights of the economy', by which he meant large-scale industry, banking and foreign trade. He added: 'We are prepared to let the peasants have their little bit of capitalism as long as we keep the power.'

Lenin's realism demanded that political theory take second place to economic need. It was this that troubled the members of the Party, such as Trotsky, Bukharin and **Preobrazhensky**, who had welcomed the repressive measures of War Communism as the proper revolutionary strategy for the Bolsheviks to follow. To their mind, bashing the peasants was exactly what the Bolsheviks should be doing since it advanced the Revolution. It disturbed them, therefore, that the peasants were being given in to and that capitalist ways were being tolerated. Trotsky described NEP as 'the first sign of the degeneration of Bolshevism'.

NEP became such a contentious issue among the Bolsheviks that Lenin took firm steps to prevent the Party being torn apart over it. At the same Party Congress in 1921, at which the NEP had been formally announced, he introduced a resolution 'On Party Unity', in which he condemned 'factionalism' (see page 4). This was his way of stifling criticism of government policy by Party members. Lenin's pronouncements at this critical juncture made it extremely difficult for doubting members to criticise NEP openly, since this would appear to be challenging the Party itself.

When introducing NEP in 1921, Lenin had admitted that it was a relaxing of strict socialism, but had emphasised that it was a temporary, stop-gap measure. However, at the time of his death in 1924, the question was already being asked as to how long in fact NEP was meant to last. Was it not becoming a permanent policy? The Party members who were unhappy with it saw its continuation as a betrayal of revolutionary principle. They objected to a policy which, in effect, allowed the peasants to dictate the pace of Soviet Russia's advance towards full Communism. A serious division had developed between **Left Communists** and **Right Communists**.

Although fierce disputes were to arise over the issue, initially the disagreement was simply about timing: how long should the NEP be allowed to run? However, in the power struggle of the 1920s, these minor differences deepened into questions of political correctness and Party loyalty. A rival's attitude towards the NEP might be a weakness to be exploited; if it could be established that his views indicated deviant Marxist thinking, it became possible to destroy his position in the Party.

Stalin did precisely this. He used Trotsky's attitude towards NEP as a way of undermining him. Trotsky had backed Lenin in 1921, but there were strong rumours that his support had been reluctant and that he regarded NEP as a deviation from true socialism. It was certainly the case that in 1923 Trotsky had led a group of Party

Key figure

Yevgeny Preobrazhensky (1886–1937)
Regarded as a major economic expert by the Bolsheviks, he was noted for his revolutionary writings.

Key terms

Left Communists
Party members who wanted NEP abandoned.

Right Communists
Party members who wanted NEP to continue.

members in openly criticising **Gosplan** for its 'flagrant radical errors of economic policy'. Trotsky's charge was that the government had placed the interests of the Nepmen above those of the Revolution and the Russian people. He urged a return to a much tighter state control of industry and warned that under NEP the revolutionary gains made under War Communism would be lost.

Stalin was quick to suggest to Party members who already looked on Trotsky as a disruptive force that he was, indeed, suspect. The interesting point here is that Stalin's own view of NEP was far from clear at this stage. He had loyally supported Lenin's introduction of it in 1921, but had given little indication as to whether, or how long, it should be retained after Lenin's death. He preferred to keep his own views to himself and play on the differences between his colleagues.

Modernisation

The NEP debate was one aspect of the larger question that remained unanswered at Lenin's death. How should the Soviet Union plan for the future? This would have been a demanding issue regardless of whether there had been a power struggle. What the rivalry for leadership did was to intensify the argument. The USSR was a poor country. To modernise and overcome its poverty it would have to industrialise. Recent history had shown that a strong industrial base was an absolute essential for a modern state and there was common agreement among Soviet Communists about that. The quarrel was not over whether the USSR should industrialise, but over how and at what speed.

History had further shown that the industrial expansion that had taken place in the previous century, in such countries as Germany and Britain, had relied on a ready supply of resources and the availability of capital for investment. Russia was rich in natural resources, but these had yet to be effectively exploited, and it certainly did not possess large amounts of capital. Nor could it easily borrow any: after 1917 the Bolsheviks had rejected **capitalist methods of finance**. Moreover, even if the Bolsheviks had been willing to borrow, there were few countries after 1917 willing to risk the dangers of investing in revolutionary Russia.

The only usable resource, therefore, was the Russian people themselves, 80 per cent of whom were peasants. To achieve industrialisation, it was necessary that the peasants be persuaded or forced into producing a food surplus which could then be sold abroad to raise capital for industrial investment. Both Left and Right agreed that this was the only solution, but, whereas the Right were content to rely on persuasion, the Left demanded that the peasantry be forced into line.

It was Trotsky who most clearly represented the view of the Left on this. He wanted the peasants to be coerced into co-operating. However, for him the industrialisation debate was secondary to the far more demanding question of Soviet Russia's role as the organiser of international revolution. His views on this created a wide divergence between him and Stalin, expressed in terms of a

Key question
Why was there a Left–Right division over the question of how the USSR should modernise?

Gosplan
The government body responsible for national economic planning.

Capitalist methods of finance
The system in which the owners of private capital (money) increase their wealth by making loans on which interest has to be paid later by the borrower.

Key terms

clash between the opposed notions of 'Permanent Revolution' and 'Socialism in One Country'.

'Permanent Revolution' versus 'Socialism in One Country'

'Permanent Revolution'

Key question
What were the essential features of Trotsky's concept of 'Permanent Revolution'?

What inspired Trotsky's politics was his belief in 'Permanent Revolution', which was made up of a number of key ideas:

- Revolution was not a single event but a permanent (continuous) process in which risings took place from country to country.
- The events in Russia since 1917 were simply a first step towards a worldwide revolution of the proletariat.
- Individual nations did not matter. The interests of the international working class were paramount.
- True revolutionary socialism could be achieved in the USSR only if an international uprising took place.

Trotsky believed that the USSR could not survive alone in a hostile world. With its vast peasant population and undeveloped proletariat, Russia would prove 'incapable of holding her own against conservative Europe'. He contended that the immediate task of the USSR was 'to export revolution'. That was the only way to guarantee its survival.

It should be stressed that at no point did Trotsky call for the Soviet Union to be sacrificed to some theoretical notion of world revolution. His argument was an opposite one: unless there was international revolution the Soviet Union would go under. Stalin, however, ignored the subtlety of his opponent's reasoning. He chose to portray Trotsky as someone intent on damaging the Soviet Union.

'Socialism in One Country'

Key question
What were the essential features of Stalin's notion of 'Socialism in One Country'?

Stalin countered Trotsky's notion of 'Permanent Revolution' with his own concept of 'Socialism in One Country'. He meant by this that the nation's first task was to consolidate Lenin's Revolution and the rule of the CPSU by turning the USSR into a modern state, capable of defending itself against its internal and external enemies. The Soviet Union, therefore, must work:

- to overcome its present agricultural and industrial problems by its own unaided efforts
- to go on to build a modern state, the equal of any nation in the world
- to make the survival of the Soviet Union an absolute priority, even if this meant suspending efforts to create international revolution.

Stalin used the contrast between this programme and Trotsky's to portray his rival as an enemy of the Soviet Union. Trotsky's ideas were condemned as an affront to Lenin and the Bolshevik Revolution. An image was created of Trotsky as an isolated figure, a posturing Jewish intellectual whose vague notions of international revolution threatened the security of the Soviet Union.

Trotsky's position was further weakened by the fact that throughout the 1920s the Soviet Union had a constant fear of invasion by the combined capitalist nations. Although this fear was ill-founded, the tense atmosphere it created made Trotsky's notion of the USSR's engaging in foreign revolutionary wars appear even more irresponsible. A number of historians, including E.H. Carr and Isaac Deutscher, have remarked on Stalin's ability to rally support and silence opponents at critical moments by assuming the role of the great Russian patriot concerned with saving the nation from the grave dangers threatening it.

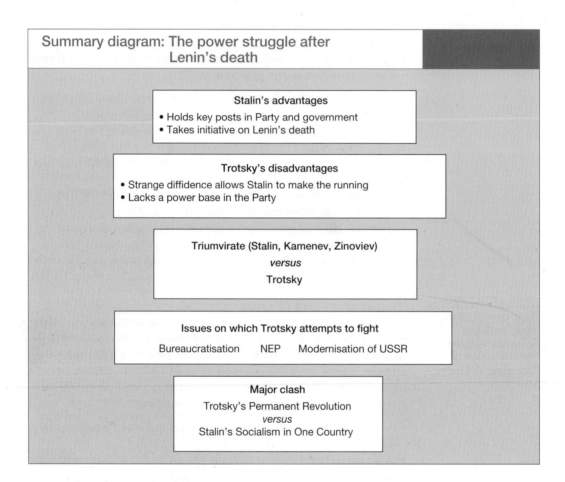

Summary diagram: The power struggle after Lenin's death

Stalin's advantages
- Holds key posts in Party and government
- Takes initiative on Lenin's death

Trotsky's disadvantages
- Strange diffidence allows Stalin to make the running
- Lacks a power base in the Party

Triumvirate (Stalin, Kamenev, Zinoviev)

versus

Trotsky

Issues on which Trotsky attempts to fight

Bureaucratisation   NEP   Modernisation of USSR

Major clash
Trotsky's Permanent Revolution
versus
Stalin's Socialism in One Country

Key question
What were the basic weaknesses of the Left in their challenge to Stalin?

Key dates

CPSU Congress votes against Trotsky: 1925

The United Opposition led by Kamenev and Zinoviev: 1925

Trotsky joined Left bloc: 1926

Key terms

'Deliver the votes'
To use one's control of the Party machine to gain majority support in key votes.

Leningrad
Petrograd had been renamed in Lenin's honour three days after his death in 1924.

United Opposition (New Opposition)
The group, led by Kamenev and Zinoviev, sometimes known as the New Opposition, who called for an end to NEP and the adoption of a rapid industrialisation programme.

3 | The Defeat of Trotsky and the Left

Trotsky's failure in the propaganda war of the 1920s meant that he was in no position to persuade either the Politburo or the Central Committee to vote for his proposals. Stalin's ability to **'deliver the votes'** in the crucial divisions was decisive. Following a vote against him in the 1925 Party Congress, Trotsky was relieved of his position as Commissar for War. Lev Kamenev and Grigory Zinoviev, the respective Chairmen of the Moscow and **Leningrad** Soviets, played a key part in this. They used their influence over the local Party organisations to ensure that it was a pro-Stalin, anti-Trotsky Congress that gathered.

Kamenev and Zinoviev

With Trotsky weakened, Stalin turned to the problem of how to deal with these two key figures, whom he now saw as potential rivals. Kamenev and Zinoviev had been motivated by a personal dislike of Trotsky, who at various times had tried to embarrass them by reminding the Party of their failure to support Lenin in October 1917. Now it was their turn to be ousted.

In the event, they created a trap for themselves. In 1925 Kamenev and Zinoviev, worried by the USSR's economic backwardness, publicly stated that it would require the victory of proletarian revolution in the capitalist nations in order for the Soviet Union to achieve socialism. Zinoviev wrote:

> When the time comes for the revolution in other countries and the proletariat comes to our aid, then we shall again go over to the offensive. For the time being we have only a little breathing space.

He called for the NEP to be abandoned, for restrictions to be reimposed on the peasants, and for enforced industrialisation.

It was understandable that Kamenev and Zinoviev, respective Party bosses in the Soviet Union's only genuinely industrial areas, Moscow and Leningrad, should have thought in these terms. Their viewpoint formed the basis of what was termed the '**United Opposition**', but it appeared to be indistinguishable from old Trotskyism. It was no surprise, therefore, when Trotsky joined his former opponents in 1926 to form a 'Trotskyite–Kamenevite–Zinovievite' opposition bloc.

Again, Stalin's control of the Party machine proved critical. The Party Congress declined to be influenced by pressure from the United Opposition. Stalin's chief backers among the Right Communists were Rykov, Tomsky and Bukharin. They and their supporters combined to outvote the bloc. Kamenev and Zinoviev were dismissed from their posts as Soviet Chairmen, to be replaced by two of Stalin's staunchest allies, Molotov in Moscow and Kirov in Leningrad. It was little surprise that soon afterwards Trotsky was expelled from both the Politburo and the Central Committee.

Trotsky exiled

Trotsky still did not admit defeat. In 1927, on the tenth anniversary of the Bolshevik rising, he tried to rally support in a direct challenge to Stalin's authority. Even fewer members of Congress than before were prepared to side with him and he was again outvoted. His complete failure led to the Congress's accepting Stalin's proposal that Trotsky be expelled from the Party altogether. An internal exile order against him in 1927 was followed two years later by total exile from the USSR.

Stalin's victory over Trotsky was not primarily a matter of ability or principle. Stalin won because Trotsky lacked a power base. Trotsky's superiority as a speaker and writer, and his greater intellectual gifts, counted for little when set against Stalin's grip on the Party machine. It is difficult to see how, after 1924, Trotsky could have ever mounted a serious challenge to his rival. Even had his own particular failings not stopped him from acting at vital moments, Trotsky never had control of the political system as it operated in Soviet Russia. Politics is the art of the possible. After 1924, all the possibilities belonged to Stalin and he used them.

Key dates

Trotsky dismissed from Central Committee: October 1927

Trotsky dismissed from Communist Party: November 1927

Trotsky sent into internal exile: January 1928

Trotsky exiled from the Soviet Union: January 1929

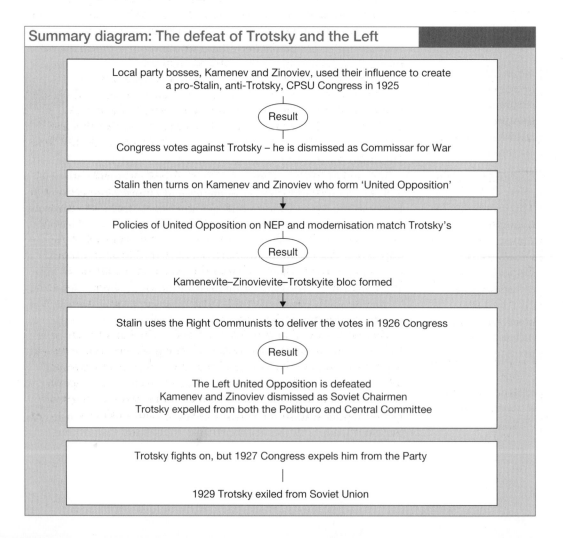

Summary diagram: The defeat of Trotsky and the Left

Local party bosses, Kamenev and Zinoviev, used their influence to create a pro-Stalin, anti-Trotsky, CPSU Congress in 1925

Result

Congress votes against Trotsky – he is dismissed as Commissar for War

Stalin then turns on Kamenev and Zinoviev who form 'United Opposition'

Policies of United Opposition on NEP and modernisation match Trotsky's

Result

Kamenevite–Zinovievite–Trotskyite bloc formed

Stalin uses the Right Communists to deliver the votes in 1926 Congress

Result

The Left United Opposition is defeated
Kamenev and Zinoviev dismissed as Soviet Chairmen
Trotsky expelled from both the Politburo and Central Committee

Trotsky fights on, but 1927 Congress expels him from the Party

1929 Trotsky exiled from Soviet Union

Key question
What was the attitude of the Right towards NEP and industrialisation?

4 | The Defeat of the Right

Although Stalin's victory over the Right Opposition is best studied as a feature of his industrialisation programme (see page 44), it is important also to see it as the last stage in the consolidation of his authority over the Party and over the USSR. The defeat of the Right marks the end of any serious attempt to limit his power. From the late 1920s to his death in 1953 he would become increasingly dictatorial.

The major representatives of the Right were Rykov, Tomsky and Bukharin, the three who had loyally served Stalin in his outflanking of Trotsky and the Left. Politically the Right were by no means as challenging to Stalin as the Trotskyite bloc had been. What made Stalin move against them was that they stood in the way of the industrial and agricultural schemes that he began to implement in 1928.

Collectivisation and industrialisation

Historians are uncertain as to when Stalin finally decided that the answer to the Soviet Union's growth problem was to impose **collectivisation** and **industrialisation**. It is unlikely to have been an early decision; the probability is that it was another piece of opportunism. Having defeated the Left politically, he may then have felt free to adopt their economic policies.

Some scholars have suggested that in 1928 Stalin became genuinely concerned about the serious grain shortage and decided that the only way to avoid a crisis was to resort to the drastic methods of collectivisation. It no longer mattered that this had been the very solution that the Left had advanced, since they were now scattered.

For some time it had been the view of Bukharin and the Right that it was unnecessary to force the pace of industrialisation in the USSR. They argued that it would be less disruptive to let industry develop its own momentum. The state should assist, but it should not direct. Similarly, the peasants should not be controlled and oppressed; this would make them resentful and less productive. The Right agreed that it was from the land that the means of financing industrialisation would have to come, but they stressed that, by offering the peasants the chance to become prosperous, far more grain would be produced for sale abroad.

Bukharin argued in the Politburo and at the Party Congress in 1928 that Stalin's aggressive policy of state **grain procurements** was counter-productive. He declared that there were alternatives to these repressive policies. Bukharin was prepared to state openly what everybody knew, but was afraid to admit: Stalin's programme was no different from the one that Trotsky had previously advocated.

Key terms

Collectivisation
The taking over by the Soviet state of the land and property previously owned by the peasants, accompanied by the requirement that the peasants now live and work communally.

Industrialisation
The introduction of a vast scheme for the building of factories which would produce heavy goods such as iron and steel.

Grain procurements
Enforced collections of fixed quotas of grain from the peasants.

Weaknesses of the Right

The Right suffered from a number of weaknesses, which Stalin was able to exploit: these related to their ideas, their organisation and their support.

Ideas

- Their economic arguments were not unsound, but, in the taut atmosphere of the late 1920s created by fear of invasion, they appeared timid and unrealistic.
- Their plea for a soft line with the peasants did not accord with the Party's needs. What the threatening times required was a dedicated resistance to the enemies of Revolution both within the USSR and outside.
- Stalin was able to suggest that the Right were guilty of underestimating the crisis facing the Party and the Soviet Union. He declared that it was a time for closing ranks in keeping with the tradition of 1917.

Stalin showed a shrewd understanding of the mentality of Party members. The majority were far more likely to respond to the call for a return to a hard-line policy, such as had helped them survive the desperate days of the Civil War, than they were to risk the Revolution itself by untimely concessions to a peasantry that had no real place in the proletarian future. The Party of Marx and Lenin would not be well served by the policies of the Right.

Organisation

- The difficulty experienced by the Right in advancing their views was the same as that which had confronted the Left. How could they impress their ideas upon the Party while Stalin remained master of the Party's organisation?
- Bukharin and his colleagues wanted to remain good Party men and it was this sense of loyalty that weakened them in their attempts to oppose Stalin. Fearful of creating 'factionalism', they hoped that they could win the whole Party round to their way of thinking without causing deep divisions. On occasion they were sharply outspoken, Bukharin particularly so, but their basic approach was conciliatory.

All this played into Stalin's hands. Since it was largely his supporters who were responsible for drafting and distributing Party information, it was not difficult for Stalin to belittle the Right as a weak and irresponsible clique.

Support

- The Right's only substantial support lay in the trade unions, whose Central Council was chaired by Tomsky, and in the CPSU's Moscow branch where **Nicolai Uglanov** was Party secretary.
- When Stalin realised that these might be a source of opposition he acted quickly and decisively. He sent **Lazar Kaganovich** to undertake a purge of the suspect trade unionists.

Key question
Why were the Right unable to mount a successful challenge to Stalin?

Key date

Stalin attacked Right over agricultural policy: 1928

Key figures

Nicolai Uglanov (1886–1940)
An admirer and supporter of Bukharin.

Lazar Kaganovich (1893–1991)
A ruthless and ambitious young Politburo member from Ukraine.

Vyacheslav Molotov (1890–1986)
A prominent Bolshevik agitator in 1917, he became a lifelong and dedicated supporter of Stalin in home and foreign affairs. Winston Churchill, the British statesman, regarded him as an 'automaton'.

Vozhd
Russian term for a supreme leader, equivalent to *der Führer* in German.

Leaders of the Right defeated and demoted by Stalin: 1929

- The Right proved incapable of organising resistance to this political blitz. **Vyacheslav Molotov**, Stalin's faithful henchman, was dispatched to Moscow where he enlisted the support of the pro-Stalin members to achieve a similar purge of the local Party officials.

By early 1929 the Right had been trounced beyond recovery. Tomsky was no longer the national trade union leader; Uglanov had been replaced in the Moscow Party organisation; Rykov had been superseded as premier by Molotov; and Bukharin had been voted out as Chairman of the Comintern and had lost his place in the Politburo. Tomsky, Rykov and Bukharin, the main trio of 'Right Opportunists' as they were termed by the Stalinist press, were allowed to remain in the Party but only after they had publicly admitted the error of their ways. Stalin's triumph over both Left and Right was complete. Stalin was now in a position to exercise power as the new *vozhd*. The grey blank was about to become the Red tsar.

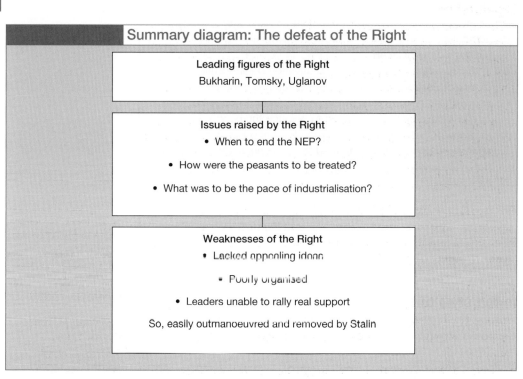

Summary diagram: The defeat of the Right

Leading figures of the Right
Bukharin, Tomsky, Uglanov

Issues raised by the Right
- When to end the NEP?
- How were the peasants to be treated?
- What was to be the pace of industrialisation?

Weaknesses of the Right
- Lacked appealing ideas
- Poorly organised
- Leaders unable to rally real support

So, easily outmanoeuvred and removed by Stalin

Study Guide: AS Questions
In the style of AQA
(a) Explain why there was a struggle for the leadership of Russia between 1924 and 1928. (12 marks)

(b) 'Stalin adopted a policy of collectivisation in 1928 simply to outwit Bukharin and the Right.' Explain why you agree or disagree with this view. (24 marks)

Exam tips
The cross-references are intended to take you straight to the material that will help you to answer the questions.

(a) For this question you would need to indicate the problems surrounding Communist leadership on Lenin's death, mentioning factionalism and the clash between the ideals and the practicalities. Key factors need to be identified, such as:

- Lenin's Testament
- Trotsky's position and actions
- Stalin's position and actions
- the position of other leading Bolsheviks
- the disputes over the NEP
- the way forward.

You should present such factors briefly. Remember that this is a short answer question and you cannot spend too long developing points. Instead you should concentrate on displaying some supported judgement about the relative weight of the factors in your answer.

(b) In this question the thrust is the motivation behind Stalin's policy of collectivisation and you may like to refer to page 29. Ideally you will also need to look at the next chapter (to page 36) for further details on this. You need to balance the economic motives for collectivisation – the need to bring Russian agriculture up to date and to feed the growing working class in the cities (and you should also include the ideological motivation, namely to get rid of the Kulaks, see chapter 3, page 37) – against the political motivation – to win the leadership struggle and dispose of the Right. Details of this struggle will be found on pages 29–31, 36–43. You will need to decide which was the more important to Stalin and argue accordingly.

In the style of Edexcel
How far do Trotsky's own misjudgements account for his failure in the power struggle which followed Lenin's death? (30 marks)

Exam tips

The cross-references are intended to take you straight to the material that will help you to answer the question.

The question is about the power struggle following Lenin's death, but it does not require you to describe that struggle. It asks you to explain why Trotsky didn't win it. The key elements to focus on in your planning are 'Trotsky's own misjudgements' and then other factors which contributed to his failure. Of course, Stalin's strengths and actions will be key here, but you should also explore the roles of Kamenev and Zinoviev.

Trotsky's misjudgements can be seen in:

- missed opportunities: to play a prominent part at Lenin's funeral (pages 17–18); to act against Stalin (pages 18–19)
- acceptance of the suppression of Lenin's Testament (page 19)
- attack on Party bureaucracy (pages 20–21)
- divisions over NEP (pages 23–24).

A more complex issue to consider is Trotsky's idea of Permanent Revolution (pages 25–26). Note Stalin's effective use of this (page 25) to weaken Trotsky's position. This is certainly evidence of Stalin's ability to create an image which undermined Trotsky. Are you going to argue that the handling of this indicates a misjudgement on Trotsky's part? It is clear that he failed in the propaganda war of the 1920s (page 27) and that this was politically significant. Did he misjudge the atmosphere (page 26)?

Stalin's strengths as a tactician and propagandist are clear from this and they are the other side of the coin, highlighting and increasing Trotsky's weaknesses. Stalin's strengths can be seen in his:

- successful undermining of Trotsky over the issue of NEP (pages 22–23)
- promotion of 'Socialism in One Country' (pages 25–26)
- exploitation of rivalries within the Left (pages 27, 28)
- exploitation of his Party position (pages 16–18, 25)
- ability to 'deliver the votes' (page 27) and the political significance of this in weakening Trotsky.

Other factors you could consider are:

- Trotsky's lack of a strong Party following (pages 19–20, 23, 24)
- opposition from Kamenev and Zinoviev (pages 19, 27).

It is easy with the benefit of hindsight to concentrate on Stalin's strengths. But, before coming to an overall conclusion, think about Trotsky's position in 1924: how strong was his position initially compared to Stalin's? Think also about those aspects where Trotsky had a choice in the period which followed, and whether any of his own decisions turned out to be important misjudgements.

3 Stalin and the Soviet Economy

POINTS TO CONSIDER
A nation's economy is vital to its development. This is
particularly true of Stalin's Russia. Stalin decided that
the USSR could not survive unless it rapidly modernised
its economy. To this end, he set about completely
reshaping Soviet agriculture and industry. This had
immense economic, social and political consequences.
These are examined here as three themes:

- Stalin's economic aims
- His collectivisation of the peasantry
- His massive industrialisation programme.

Key dates

1926	Critical resolution by Party Congress on the future of Soviet economy
1928	Collectivisation began
	Start of the First FYP (Five-Year Plan)
1932–33	Widespread famine in the USSR
1933	Start of the Second FYP
1938	Start of the Third FYP
1941	Germany invades and occupies Russia

1 | Stalin's Economic Aims

In the late 1920s Stalin decided to impose on the USSR a crash
programme of economic reform. Agriculture and industry were to
be revolutionised. The cue for the great change had been
provided in 1926 by a critical resolution of the Party Congress 'to
transform our country from an agrarian into an industrial one,
capable by its own efforts of producing the necessary means'.
Stalin planned to turn that resolution into reality.

His economic policy had one essential aim – the modernisation
of the Soviet economy – and two essential methods: collectivisation
and industrialisation. From 1928 onwards, with the introduction of
collectivisation and industrialisation, the Soviet state took over the
running of the nation's economy. Stalin's crash programme for the

Key question
What were Stalin's
motives in
revolutionising the
Soviet economy?

Critical resolution by
Party Congress on
the future of Soviet
economy: 1926

Key date

Efficient farming, so ran the argument, would have two vital results. It would create surplus food supplies that could be sold abroad to raise capital for Soviet industry. It would also decrease the number of rural workers needed and so release workers for the new factories.

The Kulaks

Key question
What was Stalin's motivation in persecuting the Kulaks?

When introducing collectivisation in 1928, Stalin claimed that it was 'voluntary', the free and eager choice of the peasants. But in truth it was forced on a very reluctant peasantry. In a major propaganda offensive, he identified a class of '**Kulaks**', who were holding back the workers' revolution by monopolising the best land and employing cheap peasant labour to farm it. By hoarding their farm produce, they kept food prices high, thus making themselves rich at the expense of the workers and poorer peasants. Unless they were broken as a class, they would prevent the modernisation of the USSR.

Key date

Collectivisation began: 1928

The concept of a Kulak class has been shown by scholars to have been a Stalinist myth. The so-called Kulaks were really only those hard-working peasants who had proved more efficient farmers than their neighbours. In no sense did they constitute the class of exploiting landowners described in Stalinist propaganda. Nonetheless, given the tradition of landlord oppression going back to tsarist times, the notion of a Kulak class proved a very powerful one and provided the grounds for the coercion of the peasantry as a whole – average and poor peasants, as well as Kulaks.

Key term

Kulaks
Rich peasants who had grown wealthy under the New Economic Policy (see page 22).

Surplus peasants and grain

As a revolutionary, Stalin had little sympathy for the peasants. Communist theory taught that the days of the peasantry as a revolutionary social force had passed. The future belonged to the urban workers. October 1917 had been the first stage in the triumph of this proletarian class. Therefore, it was perfectly fitting that the peasantry should, in a time of national crisis, bow to the demands of industrialisation. Stalin used a simple formula. The USSR needed industrial investment and manpower: the land could provide both. Surplus grain would be sold abroad to raise investment funds for industry: surplus peasants would become factory workers.

One part of the formula was correct. For generations the Russian countryside had been overpopulated, creating a chronic land shortage. The other part was a gross distortion. There was no grain surplus. Indeed, the opposite was the case. Even in the best years of NEP, food production had seldom matched needs. Yet Stalin insisted that the problem was not the lack of food but its poor distribution: food shortages were the result of grain-hoarding by the rich peasants. This argument was then used to explain the urgent need for collectivisation as a way of securing adequate food supplies. It also provided the moral grounds for the onslaught on the Kulaks, who were condemned as enemies of the Soviet nation in its struggle to modernise itself in the face of international, capitalist hostility.

Members of the Komsomol (the Communist Youth League) unearthing bags of grain hidden by peasants in a cemetery near Odessa. What opportunities did such searches give for oppressing the Kulaks?

De-Kulakisation

In some regions the poorer peasants undertook 'de-Kulakisation' with enthusiasm, since it provided them with an excuse to settle old scores and to give vent to local jealousies. Land and property were seized from the minority of better-off peasants, and they and their families were physically attacked. Such treatment was often the prelude to arrest and deportation by **OGPU** anti-Kulak squads, authorised by Stalin and modelled on the gangs which had persecuted the peasants during the state-organised terror of the Civil War period (1918–20).

The renewal of terror also served as a warning to the mass of the peasantry of the likely consequences of resisting the state reorganisation of Soviet agriculture. The destruction of the Kulaks was thus an integral part of the whole collectivisation process. As a Soviet official later admitted: 'Most Party officers thought that the whole point of de-Kulakisation was its value as an administrative measure, speeding up tempos of collectivisation.'

OGPU
Succeeded the *Cheka* as the state security force. In turn it became the NKVD and then the KGB.

Key term

An anti-Kulak demonstration on a collective farm in 1930. The banner reads 'Liquidate the Kulaks as a Class'. Who was likely to have organised such a demonstration?

Key question
What were the effects of collectivisation on the peasantry?

Resistance to collectivisation

In the period between December 1929 and March 1930, nearly half the peasant farms in the USSR were collectivised. Yet peasants in their millions resisted. What amounted to civil war broke out in the countryside. The scale of the disturbances is indicated in official figures recorded for the period 1929–30:

- 30,000 arson attacks occurred.
- Organised rural mass disturbances increased by one-third from 172 to 229.

A particularly striking feature of the disturbances was the prominent role women played in them. In Okhochaya, a village in Ukraine, the following riotous scene took place. An eyewitness described how women broke into barns where the requisition squads had dumped grain seized from the peasants:

A crowd of women stormed the kolkhoz stables and barns. They cried, screamed and wailed, demanding their cows and seed back. The men stood a way off, in clusters, sullenly silent. Some of the lads had pitchforks, stakes, axes tucked in their sashes. The terrified granary man [guard] ran away; the women tore off the bolts and together with the men began dragging out the bags of seed.

Since women, as mothers and organisers of the household, were invariably the first to suffer the harsh consequences of the new agricultural system, it was they who were often the first to take action. One peasant explained in illuminatingly simple terms why his spouse was so opposed to collectivisation: 'My wife does not want to socialise our cow.' There were cases of mothers with their children being in the front line of demonstrations and of women lying down in front of the tractors and trucks sent to break up the private farms and impose collectivisation on the localities. One peasant admitted:

> We [men] dared not speak at meetings. If we said anything that the organisers didn't like, they abused us, called us *kulaks*, and even threatened to put us in prison. We let the women do the talking. If the organiser tried to stop them they made such a din that he had to call off the meeting.

The men also thought that the women would be less likely to suffer reprisals from the authorities who certainly, judging by court records, appeared reluctant initially to prosecute female demonstrators.

However, peasant resistance no matter how valiant and desperate stood no chance of stopping collectivisation. The officials and their requisition squads pressed on with their disruptive policies. Such was the turmoil in the countryside that Stalin called a halt, blaming the troubles on over-zealous officials who had become 'dizzy with success'. Many of the peasants were allowed to return to their original holdings. However, the delay was only temporary. Having cleared his name by blaming the difficulties on local officials, Stalin restarted collectivisation in a more determined, if somewhat slower, manner. By the end of the 1930s virtually the whole of the peasantry had been collectivised (see Figure 3.1).

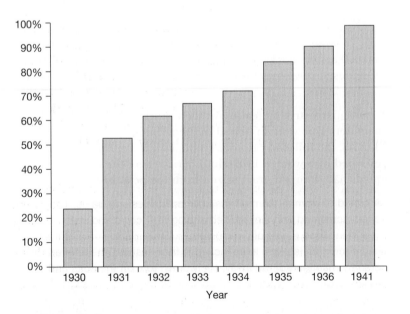

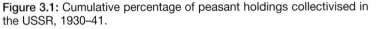

Figure 3.1: Cumulative percentage of peasant holdings collectivised in the USSR, 1930–41.

Upheaval and starvation

Behind these remarkable figures lay the story of a massive social upheaval. Bewildered and confused, the peasants either would not or could not co-operate in the deliberate destruction of their traditional way of life. The consequences were increasingly tragic. The majority of peasants ate their seed corn and slaughtered their livestock. There were no crops left to reap or animals to rear. The Soviet authorities responded with still fiercer coercion, but this simply made matters worse: imprisonment, deportation and execution could not replenish the barns or restock the herds. Special contingents of Party workers were sent from the towns to restore food production levels by working on the land themselves. But their ignorance of farming only added to the disruption. By a bitter irony, even as starvation set in, the little grain that was available was being exported as 'surplus' to obtain the foreign capital that industry demanded. By 1932 the situation on the land was catastrophic.

Table 3.1: The fall in food consumption (in kilograms per head)

	Bread	Potatoes	Meat and lard	Butter
1928	250.4	141.1	24.8	1.35
1932	214.6	125.0	11.2	0.7

Table 3.2: The fall in livestock (in millions)

	Horses	Cattle	Pigs	Sheep and goats
1928	33	70	26	146
1932	15	34	9	42

The figures in the tables refer to the USSR as a whole. In the urban areas there was more food available. Indeed, a major purpose of the grain requisition squads was to maintain adequate supplies to the industrial regions. This meant that the misery in the countryside was proportionally greater, with areas such as Ukraine and Kazhakstan suffering particularly severely. The devastation experienced by the Kazhaks can be gauged from the fact that in this period they lost nearly 90 per cent of their livestock.

National famine

Starvation, which in many parts of the Soviet Union persisted throughout the 1930s, was at its worst in the years 1932–33, when a national famine occurred. Collectivisation led to despair among the peasants. In many areas they simply stopped producing, either as an act of desperate resistance or through sheer inability to adapt to the violently enforced land system. Hungry and embittered, they made for the towns in huge numbers. It had, of course, been part of Stalin's collectivisation plan to move the peasants into the industrial regions. However, so great was the

Key question
Why could the famine of the early 1930s not be dealt with effectively?

Key date

National famine: 1932–33

migration that a system of internal passports had to be introduced in an effort to control the flow. Some idea of the horrors can be obtained from the following contemporary account:

> Trainloads of deported peasants left for the icy North, the forests, the steppes, the deserts. These were whole populations, denuded of everything; the old folk starved to death in mid-journey, new-born babes were buried on the banks of the roadside, and each wilderness had its little cross of boughs or white wood. Other populations dragging all their mean possessions on wagons, rushed towards the frontiers of Poland, Rumania, and China and crossed them – by no means intact, to be sure – in spite of the machine guns … Agricultural technicians and experts were brave in denouncing the blunders and excesses; they were arrested in thousands and made to appear in huge sabotage trials so that responsibility might be unloaded on somebody.

Official silence

Despite overwhelming evidence of the tragedy that had overtaken the USSR, the official Stalinist line was that there was no famine. In the whole of the contemporary Soviet press there were only two oblique references to it. This conspiracy of silence was of more than political significance. As well as protecting the image of Stalin the great planner, it effectively prevented the introduction of measures to remedy the distress. Since the famine did not officially exist, Soviet Russia could not publicly take steps to relieve it. For the same reason, it could not appeal, as had been done during an earlier **Russian famine in 1921**, for aid from the outside world.

Thus what Isaac Deutscher, the historian and former Trotskyist, called 'the first purely man-made famine in history' went unacknowledged in order to avoid discrediting Stalin. Not for the last time, large numbers of the Soviet people were sacrificed on the altar of Stalin's reputation. There was a strong rumour that Stalin's second wife, **Nadezdha Alliluyeva**, had been driven to suicide by the knowledge that it was her husband's brutal policies that had caused the famine. Shortly before her death she had railed at Stalin: 'You are a tormentor, that's what you are. You torment your own son. You torment your wife. You torment the whole Russian people.'

The truth of Nadezdha Alliluyeva's charge has now been put beyond doubt by the findings of scholars who have examined the Soviet archives opened up after the fall of the USSR in the early 1990s. Lynne Viola in 2007 confirmed the horrific character of Stalin's treatment of the peasantry. In harrowing detail Viola described how, between 1930 and 1932, Stalin drove two million peasants into internal exile as slave labourers, a quarter of that number dying of hunger and exposure. Viola's work, which built upon the pioneering studies of Robert Conquest, the first major

Key term

Russian famine, 1921
So severe had been the famine of 1921 that Lenin had had reluctantly to accept some $60 million worth of aid from the American Relief Association.

Key figure

Nadezdha Alliluyeva (1902–32)
Stalin's second wife; it has been suggested that Stalin's grief and desolation at her suicide help to explain why he became increasingly embittered and unfeeling towards other people.

Key figure

Nikita Khrushchev
(1894–1971)
Leader of the Soviet
Union, 1956–64.

Western historian to chart Stalin's brutalities, serves as a belated and devastating corrective to the view advanced at the time by pro-Soviet sympathisers in the West that their hero Stalin was creating a paradise on earth. It is interesting that when **Nikita Khrushchev** launched his de-Stalinisation programme in the late 1950s (see page 128), he was careful to limit his censures to Stalin's crimes against the Communist Party. He avoided referring to his former leader's crimes against the Soviet people.

Key question
How far did
collectivisation satisfy
the Soviet Union's
economic needs?

Was collectivisation justifiable on economic grounds?

Even allowing for the occasional progressive aspect of collectivisation, such as the building and distributing of mechanised tractors, the overall picture was bleak. The mass of the peasantry had been uprooted and left bewildered. Despite severe reprisals and coercion, the peasants were unable to produce the surplus food that Stalin demanded. By 1939 Soviet agricultural productivity had barely returned to the level recorded for tsarist Russia in 1913. But the most damning consideration still remains the man-made famine, which in the 1930s killed between 10 and 15 million peasants.

However, there is another aspect worth examining. The hard fact is that Stalin's policies did force a large number of peasants to leave the land. This was a process that Russia needed. Economic historians have often stressed that there was a land crisis in Russia which predated Communism. Since the nineteenth century, land in Russia had proved incapable of supporting the growing number of people who lived unproductively on it. Unless a major shift occurred in the imbalance between urban and rural dwellers Russia would be in sustained difficulties. The nation needed to change from an agricultural and rural society to an urban and industrial one.

There is a case for arguing, therefore, that Stalin's collectivisation programme, brutally applied though it was, did answer to one of the USSR's great needs. Leaving aside questions of human suffering, the enforced migration under Stalin made economic sense. It relieved the pressure on the land and provided the workforce which enabled the industrialisation programme to be started. Perhaps all this could be summed up by saying that Stalin's aims were understandable but his methods were unacceptable. He did the wrong thing for the right reason.

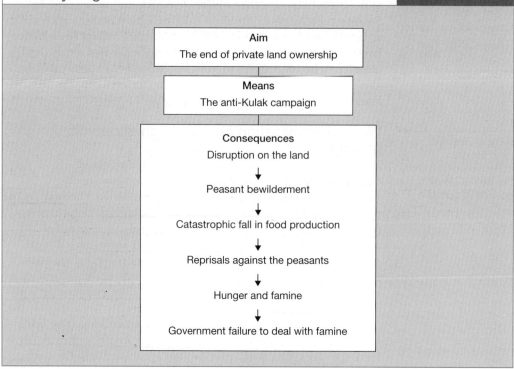

Summary diagram: Collectivisation

Aim
The end of private land ownership

Means
The anti-Kulak campaign

Consequences
Disruption on the land
↓
Peasant bewilderment
↓
Catastrophic fall in food production
↓
Reprisals against the peasants
↓
Hunger and famine
↓
Government failure to deal with famine

3 | Industrialisation

Stalin described his industrialisation plans for the USSR as an attempt to establish a war economy. He declared that he was making war on the failings of Russia's past and on the class enemies within the nation. He also claimed that he was preparing the USSR for war against its capitalist foes abroad. This was not simply martial imagery. Stalin regarded iron, steel and oil as the sinews of war. Their successful production would guarantee the strength and readiness of the nation to face its enemies.

For Stalin, therefore, industry meant heavy industry. He believed that the industrial revolutions which had made Western Europe and North America so strong had been based on iron and steel production. It followed that the USSR must adopt a similar industrial pattern in its drive towards modernisation. The difference would be that, whereas the West had taken the capitalist road, the USSR would follow the path of socialism.

Stalin had grounds for his optimism. It so happened that the Soviet industrialisation drive in the 1930s coincided with the **Depression** in the Western world. Stalin claimed that the USSR was introducing into its own economy the technical successes of Western industrialisation but was rejecting the destructive capitalist system that went with them. Socialist planning would enable the USSR to avoid the errors that had begun to undermine the Western economies.

Key question
What were Stalin's aims for Soviet industry in the 1930s?

Depression
A period of severe economic stagnation which began in the USA in 1929 and lasted throughout the 1930s. It affected the whole of the industrial world and was interpreted by Marxists as a sign of the final collapse of capitalism.

Key term

Soviet industrialisation under Stalin took the form of a series of Five-Year Plans (FYPs). Gosplan, the government body responsible for economic planning, was required by Stalin to draw up a list of quotas of production ranging across the whole of Soviet industry. The process began in 1928 and, except for the war years 1941–45, lasted until Stalin's death in 1953. In all, there were five separate Plans:

- 1st FYP   October 1928 to December 1932
- 2nd FYP   January 1933 to December 1937
- 3rd FYP   January 1938 to June 1941
- 4th FYP   January 1946 to December 1950
- 5th FYP   January 1951 to December 1955

The First Five-Year Plan

Key question
What was the purpose of the First FYP?

The term 'plan' is misleading. The First FYP laid down what was to be achieved, but did not say how it was to be done. It simply assumed the quotas would be met. What the First FYP represented, therefore, was a set of targets rather than a plan.

Key date

First FYP: 1928–32

As had happened with collectivisation, local officials and managers falsified their production figures to give the impression they had met their targets when, in fact, they had fallen short. For this reason, precise statistics for the First FYP are difficult to determine. A further complication is that three quite distinct versions of the First FYP eventually appeared.

Impressed by the apparent progress of the Plan in its early stages, Stalin encouraged the formulation of an 'optimal' Plan which reassessed targets upwards. These new quotas were hopelessly unrealistic and stood no chance of being reached. Nonetheless, on the basis of the supposed achievements of this optimal Plan the figures were revised still higher. Western analysts suggest the figures in Table 3.3 as the closest approximation to the real statistics:

Table 3.3: Industrial output

Product (in million tons)	1927–28 First Plan	1932–33 'Optimal'	1932 Revised	1932 Actual
Coal	35.0	75.0	95–105	64.0
Oil	11.7	21.7	40–55	21.4
Iron ore	6.7	20.2	24–32	12.1
Pig iron	3.2	10.0	15–16	6.2

Propaganda and collective effort

Key question
How did the Soviet people respond to Stalin's call?

The importance of these figures should not be exaggerated. At the time it was the grand design, not the detail, that mattered. The Plan was a huge propaganda project, which aimed at convincing the Soviet people that they were personally engaged in a vast industrial enterprise. By their own efforts, they were changing the character of the society in which they lived and providing it with the means of achieving greatness.

Nor was it all a matter of state enforcement, fierce though that was. Among the young especially, there was an enthusiasm and a commitment that suggested many Soviet citizens believed they were genuinely building a new and better world. The sense of the Soviet people as masters of their own fate was expressed in the slogan, 'There is no fortress that we Bolsheviks cannot storm.' John Scott, an American Communist and one of the many pro-Soviet Western industrial advisers who came to the USSR at this time, was impressed by the mixture of idealism and coercion that characterised the early stages of Stalinist industrialisation. He described how the city of Magnitogorsk in the Urals was built from scratch:

> Within several years, half a billion cubic feet of excavation was done, forty-two million cubic feet of reinforced concrete poured, five million cubic feet of fire bricks laid, a quarter of a million tons of structured steel erected. This was done without sufficient labour, without necessary quantities of the most elementary materials. Brigades of young enthusiasts from every corner of the Soviet Union arrived in the summer of 1930 and did the groundwork of railroad and dam construction necessary. Later, groups of local peasants and herdsmen came to Magnitogorsk because of bad conditions in the villages, due to collectivisation. Many of the peasants were completely unfamiliar with industrial tools and processes. A colony of several hundred foreign engineers and specialists, some of whom made as high as one hundred dollars a day, arrived to advise and direct the work.
>
> From 1928 until 1932 nearly a quarter of a million people came to Magnitogorsk. About three quarters of these new arrivals came of their own free will seeking work, bread-cards, better conditions. The rest came under compulsion.

'The Five-Year Plan' – a propaganda wall poster of the 1930s, depicting Stalin as the heroic creator of a powerful, industrialised, Soviet Union. He is overcoming the forces of religion, international capitalism, and Russian conservatism and backwardness.

Cultural revolution

The term 'cultural revolution' is an appropriate description of the significance of what was taking place under Stalin's leadership. Two renowned Western analysts of Soviet affairs, Alec Nove and Sheila Fitzpatrick, have stressed this aspect. They see behind the economic changes of this period a real attempt being made to create a new type of individual, *Homo sovieticus* (Soviet man), as if a new species had come into being. Stalin told a gathering of Soviet writers that they should regard themselves as 'engineers of the human soul' (see page 103).

Successes and achievements

Key question
How far did the First FYP achieve its objectives?

No matter how badly the figures may have been rigged at the time, the First FYP was an extraordinary achievement overall. The output of coal and iron and the generation of electricity all increased in huge proportions. The production of steel and chemicals was less impressive, while the output of finished textiles actually declined.

A striking feature of the Plan was the low priority it gave to improving the material lives of the Soviet people. No effort was made to reward the workers by providing them with affordable consumer goods. Living conditions actually deteriorated in this period. Accommodation in the towns and cities remained sub-standard. The Soviet authorities' neglect of basic social needs was not accidental. The Plan had never been intended to raise living standards. Its purpose was collective, not individual. It called for sacrifice on the part of the workers in the construction of a socialist state, which would be able to sustain itself economically and militarily against the enmity of the outside world.

Resistance and sabotage

Key question
Why was there so little resistance to the FYP?

It was Stalin's presentation of the FYP as a defence of the USSR against international hostility that enabled him to brand resistance to the Plan as 'sabotage'. A series of public trials of industrial 'wreckers', including a number of foreign workers, was staged to impress upon the Party and the masses the futility of protesting against the industrialisation programme. In 1928, in a prelude to the First FYP, Stalin claimed to have discovered an anti-Soviet conspiracy among the mining engineers of Shakhty in the Donbass region. Their subsequent public trial was intended to frighten the workers into line. It also showed that the privileged position of the skilled workers, the 'bourgeois experts', was to be tolerated no longer.

This attack upon the experts was part of a pattern in the First FYP which stressed quantity at the expense of quality. The push towards sheer volume of output was intended to prove the correctness of Stalin's grand economic schemes. Sheila Fitzpatrick has described this as being an aspect of Stalin's **'gigantomania'**, his love of mighty building projects like canals, bridges and docks, which he regarded as proof that the USSR was advancing to greatness.

Key term

'Gigantomania'
The worship of size for its own sake.

Stalin's emphasis on gross output may also be interpreted as shrewd thinking on his part. He knew that the untrained peasants who now filled the factories would not turn immediately into skilled workers. It made sense, therefore, at least in the short term, to ignore the question of quality and to stress quantity. The result very often was that machines, factories and even whole enterprises were ruined because of the workers' lack of basic skills.

Stalin was seemingly untroubled by this. His notions of industrial 'saboteurs' and 'wreckers' allowed him to place the blame for poor quality and under-production on managers and workers who were not prepared to play their proper part in rebuilding the nation. He used OGPU agents and Party **cadres** to terrorise the workforce. 'Sabotage' became a blanket term used to denounce anyone considered not to be pulling his weight. The simplest errors, such as being late for work or mislaying tools, could lead to such a charge.

At a higher level, those factory managers or foremen who did not meet their production quotas might find themselves on public trial as enemies of the Soviet state. In such an atmosphere of fear and recrimination, doctoring official returns and inflating output figures became normal practice. Everybody at every level engaged in a huge game of pretence. This was why Soviet statistics for industrial growth were so unreliable and why it was possible for Stalin to claim in mid-course that, since the First FYP had already met its initial targets, it would be shortened to a four-year plan. In Stalin's industrial revolution, appearances were everything. This was where the logic of 'gigantomania' had led.

Stalin – the master-planner?

The industrial policies of this time had been described as 'the Stalinist blue-print' or 'Stalin's economic model'. Modern scholars are, however, wary of using such terms. Norman Stone, for example, interprets Stalin's policies not as far-sighted strategy but as 'simply putting one foot in front of the other as he went along'. Despite the growing tendency in all official Soviet documents of the 1930s to include a fulsome reference to Stalin, the master-planner, there was in fact very little planning from the top.

It is true that Stalin's government exhorted, cajoled and bullied the workers into ever greater efforts towards ever greater production. But such planning as there was occurred not at national but at local level. It was the regional and site managers who, struggling desperately to make sense of the instructions they were given from on high, formulated the actual schemes for reaching their given production quotas. This was why it was so easy for Stalin and his Kremlin colleagues to accuse lesser officials of sabotage while themselves avoiding any taint of incompetence.

Key term

Cadres
Party members who were sent into factories and onto construction sites to spy and report back on managers and workers.

Key question
How far was the First FYP planned from the top?

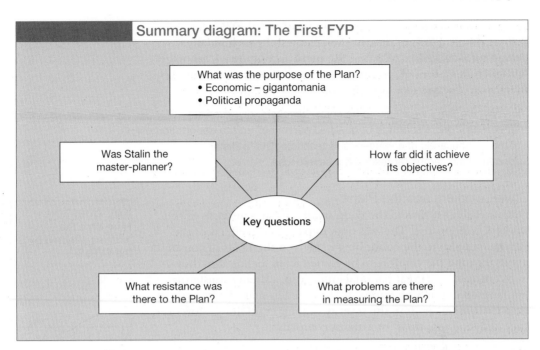

Summary diagram: The First FYP

What was the purpose of the Plan?
• Economic – gigantomania
• Political propaganda

Was Stalin the master-planner?

How far did it achieve its objectives?

Key questions

What resistance was there to the Plan?

What problems are there in measuring the Plan?

Key question
What were the main strengths and weaknesses of the Second and Third Five-Year Plans?

Key dates

Second FYP:
1933–37

Third FYP:
1938–41

The Second and Third Five-Year Plans

Although the Second and Third FYPs were modelled on the pattern of the First, the targets set for them were more realistic. Nevertheless, they still revealed the same lack of co-ordination that had characterised the First. Over-production occurred in some parts of the economy, under-production in others, which frequently led to whole branches of industry being held up for lack of vital supplies. For example, some projects had too little timber at times, while at other times enough timber but insufficient steel. Spare parts were hard to come by, which often meant broken machines standing unrepaired and idle for long periods.

The hardest struggle was to maintain a proper supply of materials; this often led to fierce competition between regions and sectors of industry, all of them anxious to escape the charge of failing to achieve their targets. As a result there was hoarding of resources and a lack of co-operation between the various parts of the industrial system. Complaints about poor standards, carefully veiled so as not to appear critical of Stalin and the Plan, were frequent. What successes there were occurred again in heavy industry, where the Second FYP began to reap the benefit of the creation of large-scale plants under the First Plan.

Scapegoats

The reluctance to tell the full truth hindered genuine industrial growth. Since no one was willing to admit there was an error in the planning, faults went unchecked until serious breakdowns occurred. There then followed the familiar search for scapegoats.

It was during the period of the Second and Third FYPs that Stalin's political purges were at their fiercest. In such an all-pervading atmosphere of terror the mere accusation of 'sabotage' was taken as a proof of guilt. Productivity suffered as a result. As Alec Nove observes (see page 54):

> Everywhere there were said to be spies, wreckers, diversionists. There was a grave shortage of qualified personnel, so the deportation of many thousands of engineers and technologists to distant concentration camps represented a severe loss.

Soviet workers and the Plans

Despite Stalin's claims to the contrary, the living standards of the workers failed to rise. This was due, in part, to the effects of the famine, but also to the continuing neglect in the Plans of consumer goods. Beyond the comfort to be gained from feeling that they were engaged in a great national enterprise, a theme constantly emphasised in the Soviet press, there were few material rewards to help the workers endure the severity of their conditions. Moreover, they had to accept their lot without complaint.

The Stakhanovite movement, 1935

The Party's control of newspapers, cinema and radio meant that only a favourable view of the Plans was ever presented. The official line was that all was well and the workers were happy. Support for this claim was provided by the Stakhanovite movement, after **Alexei Stakhanov**, a miner in the Donbass region. In August 1935 it was officially claimed that Stakhanov had singly cut over 100 tons of coal in one five-hour shift, which was more than 14 times his required quota.

Stakhanov's reported feat was seized on by the authorities as a glorious example of what was possible in a Soviet Union guided by the great and wise Joseph Stalin. Miners, indeed workers everywhere, were urged to match Stakhanov's dedication by similar '**storming**'. It all seemed very fine but it proved more loss than gain. While some 'Stakhanovite' groups produced more output in factories and on farms, this was achieved only by their being given privileged access to tools and supplies and by changing work plans to accommodate them. The resulting disruption led to a loss of production overall in those areas where the movement was at its most enthusiastic.

Workers' rights

After 1917, the Russian trade unions had become powerless. In Bolshevik theory, in a truly socialist state such as Russia now was, there was no distinction between the interests of government and those of the workers. Therefore, there was no longer any need for a separate trade union movement. In 1920 Trotsky had taken violent steps to destroy the independence of the unions and bring them directly under Bolshevik control. The result was that after 1920 the unions were simply the means by which the Bolshevik government enforced its requirements upon the workers.

Key question
How were the workers affected by the FYPs?

Key figure

Alexei Stakhanov (1906–77)
As was later admitted by the Soviet authorities, though not until 1988, his achievement had been grossly exaggerated. He had not worked on his own but as part of a team, which had been supplied with the best coal-cutting machines available.

Key term

Storming
An intensive period of work to meet a highly demanding set target. Despite the propaganda with which it was introduced, storming proved a very inefficient form of industrial labour and was soon abandoned.

Under Stalin's industrialisation programme any vestige of workers' rights disappeared. Strikes were prohibited and the traditional demands for better pay and conditions were regarded as selfishly inappropriate in a time of national crisis. A code of 'labour discipline' was drawn up, demanding maximum effort and output; failure to conform was punishable by a range of penalties from loss of wages to imprisonment in forced labour camps. On paper, wages improved during the Second FYP, but in real terms, since there was food rationing and high prices, living standards were lower in 1937 than they had been in 1928.

Living and working conditions

Throughout the period of the FYPs, the Soviet government asserted that the nation was under siege. It claimed that unless priority was given to defence needs, the very existence of the USSR was at risk. Set against such a threat, workers' material interests were of little significance. For workers to demand improved conditions at a time when the Soviet Union was fighting for survival was unthinkable: they would be betraying the nation. It was small wonder, then, that food remained scarce and expensive and severe overcrowding persisted.

There was money available, but the government spent it not on improving social conditions but on armaments. Between 1933 and 1937, defence expenditure rose from 4 to 17 per cent of the overall industrial budget. By 1940, under the terms of the Third FYP, which renewed the commitment to heavy industrial development, a third of the USSR's government spending was on arms.

Key question
How successful had Stalin's economic reforms been by 1940?

Strengths of the reforms

In judging the scale of Stalin's achievement it is helpful to cite such statistics relating to industrial output during the period of the first three FYPs as are reliable. The data in Table 3.4 are drawn from the work of the economic historian E. Zaleski, whose findings are based on careful analysis of Soviet and Western sources.

Table 3.4: Industrial output during the first three FYPs

	1927	1930	1932	1935	1937	1940
Coal (million tons)	35	60	64	100	128	150
Steel (million tons)	3	5	6	13	18	18
Oil (million tons)	12	17	21	24	26	26
Electricity (million kWh)	18	22	20	45	80	90

The figures indicate a remarkable increase in production overall. In a little over 12 years, coal production had grown five-fold, steel six-fold, and oil output had more than doubled. Perhaps the most impressive statistic is the one showing that electricity generation had quintupled. These four key products provided the basis for the military economy which enabled the USSR not only to survive four years of German occupation but eventually to amass sufficient resources to turn the tables and drive the German army out of

Soviet territory. The climax of this was the Soviet invasion and defeat of Germany in May 1945.

Weaknesses of the reforms

Stalin's economic reforms succeeded only in the traditional areas of heavy industry. In those sectors where unskilled and forced labour could be easily used, as in the building of large projects such as factories, bridges, refineries and canals, the results were impressive. However, the Soviet economy itself remained unbalanced. Stalin gave little thought to developing an overall economic strategy. Nor were modern industrial methods adopted. Old, wasteful techniques, such as using massed labour rather than efficient machines, continued to be used. Vital financial and material resources were squandered.

Stalin's love of what he called 'the Grand Projects of Communism' meant no real attention was paid to producing quality goods that could then be profitably sold abroad to raise the money the USSR so badly needed. He loved to show off to foreign visitors the great projects that were either completed or under construction. Two enterprises of which he was especially proud were the city of Magnitogorsk (see page 46) and the **White Sea Canal**. Yet, it was all vainglorious. Despite Stalin's boasts and the adulation with which he was regarded by foreign sympathisers, the simple fact remained that his policies had deprived the Soviet Union of any chance of genuinely competing with the modernising economies of Europe and the USA.

Moreover, his schemes failed to increase agricultural productivity or to raise the living standards of the Soviet workers. Stalin's neglect of agriculture, which continued to be deprived of funds since it was regarded as wholly secondary to the needs of industry, proved very damaging. The lack of agricultural growth resulted in constant food shortages which could be met only by buying foreign supplies. This drained the USSR's limited financial resources.

Despite the official veneration of Stalin for his great diplomatic triumph in achieving the non-aggression pact with Nazi Germany in August 1939 (see page 86) there was no relaxation within the Soviet Union of the war atmosphere. Indeed, the conditions of the ordinary people became even harsher. An official decree of 1940 empowered Stalin's government to encroach even further on workers' liberties. Direction of labour, enforced settlement of undeveloped areas, and severe penalties for slacking and absenteeism: these were some of the measures imposed under the decree.

In 1941, when the German invasion effectively destroyed the Third FYP, the conditions of the Soviet industrial workers were marginally lower than in 1928. Yet whatever the hardship of the workers, the fact was that in 1941 the USSR was economically strong enough to engage in an ultimately successful military struggle of unprecedented duration and intensity. In Soviet propaganda, this was what mattered, not minor questions of living standards. The USSR's triumph over Nazism would later be claimed as the ultimate proof of the wisdom of Stalin's enforced industrialisation programme.

Key term

White Sea Canal
In fact three canals linking Leningrad with the White Sea; built predominantly by forced labourers, who died in their thousands, the canal proved practically worthless since it was hardly used after construction.

Key date

German invasion and occupation of Russia: June 1941

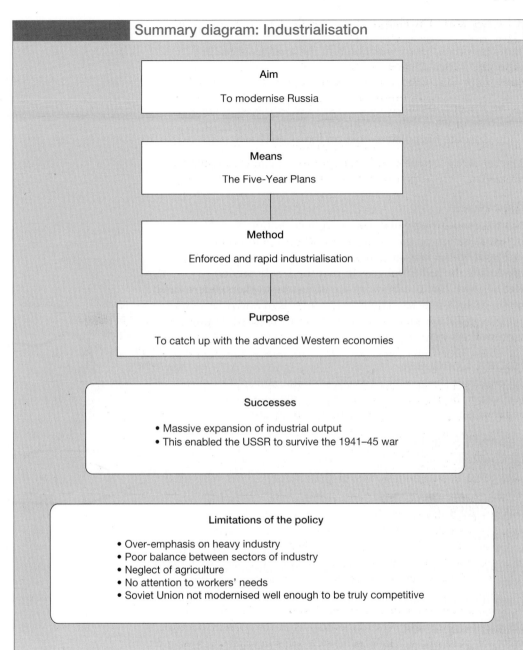

Summary diagram: Industrialisation

Aim

To modernise Russia

Means

The Five-Year Plans

Method

Enforced and rapid industrialisation

Purpose

To catch up with the advanced Western economies

Successes

• Massive expansion of industrial output
• This enabled the USSR to survive the 1941–45 war

Limitations of the policy

• Over-emphasis on heavy industry
• Poor balance between sectors of industry
• Neglect of agriculture
• No attention to workers' needs
• Soviet Union not modernised well enough to be truly competitive

4 | The Key Debate

Many historians have contributed to the analysis of Stalin's economic policies, which remain a lively area of discussion. The central question which scholars address is:

Did the economic policies benefit the Soviet Union and its people or were they introduced by Stalin primarily to consolidate his political hold on the USSR?

The following are the views of some of the main contributors to the debate.

Alec Nove

Nove argued strongly that Stalin's collectivisation and industrialisation programmes were bad economics. They caused upheaval on the land and misery to the peasants without producing the industrial growth that the USSR needed. Furthermore, the condition of the industrial workers deteriorated under Stalin's policies. The living standards of Soviet factory workers in 1953 were barely higher than in 1928, while those of farm workers were actually lower than in 1913.

Robert Conquest

An especially sharp critic of Stalin's totalitarianism, Conquest remarked: 'Stalinism is one way of attaining industrialisation, just as cannibalism is one way of attaining a high protein diet.'

Leonard Shapiro

He contended that had the industrial growth under the tsars continued uninterrupted beyond 1914, it would have reached no less a level of expansion by 1941 than that achieved by Stalin's terror strategy.

Norman Stone

Stone has supported Shapiro's view by arguing that without the expertise and basic industrial structures that already existed in Russia before 1917, the Five-Year Plans would have been unable to reach the level of success that they did.

Sheila Fitzpatrick

Fitzpatrick broadly agreed with Nove's and Conquest's criticisms; she added that Stalin's 'gigantomania', his obsession with large-scale projects, distorted the economy at a critical time calling out for proper investment and planning. She laid emphasis on Stalin's failure to improve Soviet living standards:

Despite its promises of future abundance and the massive propaganda that surrounded its achievements, the Stalinist regime did little to improve the life of its people in the 1930s …

Sheila Fitzpatrick also stressed, however, that Stalin's policies need to be seen in a broad social and political context. Harsh though Stalin was, he was trying to bring stability to a Soviet Russia that had known only turmoil and division since 1917.

Dmitri Volkogonov

Volkogonov, who saw things at first hand as a soldier and administrator in 1930s Russia, suggested that the real purpose of Stalin's policies was only incidentally economic: the Soviet leader was aiming at removing all opposition to himself by making his economic policies a test of loyalty. To question his plans was to challenge his authority.

Peter Gattrell

An interesting viewpoint was offered by Peter Gattrell, who built on the arguments first put forward by E.H. Carr. He acknowledged that Stalin was certainly severe and destructive in his treatment of people, but pointed out that the outcome of collectivisation and industrialisation was an economy strong enough to sustain the USSR through four years of the most demanding of modern wars. Gattrell suggested that, hard though it is for the Western liberal mind to accept, it may be that Russia could not have been modernised by any other methods except those used by Stalin.

David Hoffman

Hoffman offers a strongly contrary argument by suggesting that Stalin's use of coercion in seeking economic and social change proved both inhumane and ineffective:

> Social change must be gradual and consensual if it is to succeed. Even if violence achieves superficial change, it does not permanently transform the way people think and act. Moreover in the Soviet case the means and ends were themselves in contradiction. State coercion by its very nature could not create social harmony. The arrest and execution of millions of people only sowed hatred, mistrust and disharmony in Soviet society.

Terry Martin

Martin has also seen an essential contradiction in Stalin's economic policies. He has pointed out a basic paradox in Stalin's attempt to enforce modernisation on the Soviet Union. Martin notes that, contrary to what the Soviet leader intended, Stalin's methods did not take the USSR forward but returned it to **neo-traditionalist** ways. In its attempt to get rid of market forces and competition, Stalin's programme of collectivisation and industrialisation, as actually practised, became as heavily dependent on *blat* as ever tsarist capitalism had been.

Key terms

Neo-traditionalism
A return to customary, established ways of doing things.

Blat
Russian word for a system that operates through bribes, favours and connections.

Robert Service

Stalin's outstanding biographer makes the following succinct assessment of the effects of his subject's collectivisation and industrialisation programme by 1940:

> Disruption was everywhere in the economy. Ukraine, south Russia, and Kazakhstan were starving The Gulag [Russia's labour camp system] heaved with prisoners. Nevertheless the economic transformation was no fiction. The USSR under Stalin's rule had been pointed decisively in the direction of becoming an industrial, urban society. This had been his great objective. His gamble was paying off for him, albeit not for millions of victims. Magnitogorsk and the White Sea Canal were constructed at the expense of the lives of Gulag convicts, Ukrainian peasants and even undernourished, overworked factory labourers.

Some key books in the debate:

E.H. Carr, *A History of Soviet Russia* (Macmillan, 1979)

Robert Conquest, *The Great Terror: Stalin's Purge of the Thirties* (Penguin, 1971)

Robert Conquest, *Harvest of Sorrow* (Macmillan, 1988)

Sheila Fitzpatrick, *The Cultural Front: Power and Culture in Revolutionary Russia* (Cornell, 1992)

Sheila Fitzpatrick, *Everyday Stalinism: Ordinary Life in Extraordinary Times: Soviet Russia in the 1930s* (OUP, 1999)

Sheila Fitzpatrick (ed.), *Stalinism: New Directions* (Routledge, 2000)

Peter Gattrell, *Under Command: The Soviet Economy 1924–53* (Routledge, 1992)

David L. Hoffman, *Stalinist Values: The Cultural Norms of Soviet Modernity* (Cornell, 2003)

Alec Nove, *An Economic History of the USSR* (Penguin, 1972)

Alec Nove, *Stalinism and After* (Allen and Unwin, 1975)

Robert Service, *Stalin: A Biography* (Macmillan, 2004)

Norman Stone, *The Eastern Front* (Hodder & Stoughton, 1975)

Robert Tucker, *Stalinism: Essays in Historical Interpretation* (WW Norton, 1999)

Lynne Viola, *The Unknown Gulag: The Lost World of Stalin's Special Settlements* (OUP, 2007)

Dmitri Volkogonov, *The Rise and Fall of the Soviet Empire* (HarperCollins, 1998)

Dmitri Volkogonov, *Stalin: Triumph and Tragedy* (Weidenfeld and Nicolson, 1991)

Study Guide: AS Questions

In the style of AQA

(a) Explain why Stalin introduced the First Five-Year Plan in
October 1928. (12 marks)

(b) 'Stalin's economic changes had failed to transform the Soviet
economy by 1941.' Explain why you agree or disagree with this
view. (24 marks)

Exam tips

*The cross-references are intended to take you straight to the material
that will help you to answer the questions.*

(a) For this question you are looking for a range of reasons. A good
answer should distinguish between the political, ideological and
economic motives, as well as the general and more specific
considerations.

- A political reason might be to clinch Stalin's struggle for the
leadership (see previous chapter).
- An ideological motive would be to ensure state control and to
carry through Marxist, anti-capitalist principles.
- The economic motives would include catching up with the
West and strengthening the USSR (in order to be able to resist
the West).

More specifically you might comment on why he chose to set
targets and a time limit. You might argue that these were
necessary to promote rapid change and also to permit greater
state control, with an opportunity to set an example of those who
responded and to punish those who failed to meet demands.

(b) For this question you will need to re-read the material in this
chapter and in particular the assessment on pages 47–53. You
should identify the ways in which Stalin's changes had and had
not transformed the economy and should decide on whether you
wish to agree or disagree before you begin writing. In support of
his success you could cite the statistics (page 51) and explain
some of the major industrial achievements. However, you need to
balance such successes against the sectors which showed slower
advance, such as agriculture. Please note, however, this question
does not require a discussion of the social impact of economic
change.

In the style of Edexcel

How far is it accurate to describe Stalin's policy of collectivisation as a failure?   (30 marks)

> ### Exam tips
>
> *The cross-references are intended to take you straight to the material that will help you to answer the question.*
>
> Questions which ask you for a judgement about failure or success are not as easy to plan as ones which ask you to analyse the causes of an event or situation. In a question like this one, you will need to be clear what criteria you are going to apply in order to say something failed. Be careful not to get led into simply describing the process of collectivisation. You should also apply more than one criterion of success/failure. You have learnt from this chapter what a huge cost in human suffering accompanied collectivisation – but be wary of making that your only criterion by which to judge. You must consider economic as well as social or political criteria. In reaching a judgement, you will need to be clear about what the aims of collectivisation were and take them into account as part of the process of deciding whether or not it was, overall, a failure.
>
> You could develop a plan with the key aims of collectivisation (pages 36–44) at the top of your page and then sort the outcomes of the policy of collectivisation into two columns, depending on whether or not those outcomes indicate that the aims were being met.
>
> Into which column will you put information about the following? How will you group and organise the information? Remember that from a single heading, you may find material which belongs in both columns.
>
> - implementation of collectivisation (pages 36–37)
> - mechanisation (page 37)
> - resistance (pages 39–40)
> - agricultural productivity (pages 41–42)
> - famine (pages 41–42)
> - population movement (pages 41, 42–43)
> - the needs of industry (pages 34, 36).
>
> What is your decision? Overall can you describe this as a policy which failed? Read pages 54–56 carefully before coming to a decision.

4 Stalin's Terror State

POINTS TO CONSIDER

With his defeat by 1929 of the Left and Right Bolsheviks, Stalin had achieved personal power in the Soviet Union. He went on to turn that power into absolute control by a series of purges that continued until his death in 1953. In this chapter these are examined as:

- The early purges
- The post-Kirov purges, 1934–36
- The Great Purge, 1936–39
- The later purges, 1941–53
- The purges as a study in Stalin's use of power.

Key dates

1932	Trial of the Ryutin group
1933	Purges began under Yezhov's direction
1933–34	Legal system brought under Stalin's control
1934	Assassination of Kirov
	Intensification of the purges under Yagoda
1935	Yezhov, Vyshinsky and Beria took over organising the purges
1936–39	The 'Great Purge' of the Party, the Army and the people
1937–38	The Yezhovschina persecutions in the localities
1941–45	Purges removed those accused of undermining the war effort
1945	Purging of Soviet people believed to have supported Germany
1949	The 'Leningrad Affair' led to a further purge of the Party
1953	The 'Doctors' Plot', which began a purge of the medical profession, was ended by the death of Stalin

1 | The Early Purges

Having become the *vozhd* (supreme leader) of the Soviet Union by 1929, Stalin spent the rest of his life consolidating and extending his authority. The purges were his principal weapon for achieving this. The Stalinist purges, which began in 1932, were not unprecedented. Under Lenin, in the early 1920s, tens of thousands of 'anti-Bolsheviks' had been imprisoned in labour camps. Public trials, such as the Shakhty affair, had been held during the early stages of the First Five-Year Plan as a way of exposing industrial 'saboteurs' (see page 47).

However, even at this early stage, prosecutions had not been restricted to industrial enemies. In 1932, the trial of the **Ryutin group** had taken place. Ryutin and his supporters were publicly tried and expelled from the Party. This was the prelude to the first major purge of the CPSU by Stalin. Between 1933 and 1934 nearly one million members, over a third of the total membership, were excluded from the Party on the grounds that they were 'Ryutinites'. The purge was organised by **Nicolai Yezhov**, Chief of the Control Commission, the branch of the Central Committee responsible for Party discipline.

Nature of the early purges

At the beginning, Party purges were not as violent or as deadly as they later became. The usual procedure was to oblige members to hand in their **Party card** for checking, at which point any suspect individuals would not have their cards returned to them. This amounted to expulsion since, without cards, members were denied access to all Party activities. Furthermore, they and their families then lost their privileges in regard to employment, housing and food rations. The threat of expulsion was enough to force members to conform to official Party policy.

Under such a system, it became progressively difficult to mount effective opposition. Despite this, attempts were made in the early 1930s to criticise Stalin, as the Ryutin affair illustrates. These efforts were ineffectual, but they led Stalin to believe that organised resistance to him was still possible.

The purges intensify

The year 1934 is an important date in Stalin's rise to absolute authority. It marks the point at which the purges he began developed into systematic terrorising not of obvious political opponents but of colleagues and Party members. It is difficult to explain precisely why Stalin initiated such a terror. Historians accept that they are dealing with behaviour that sometimes went beyond reason and logic. Stalin was deeply suspicious by nature and suffered from increasing **paranoia** as he grew older. Right up to his death in 1953 he continued to believe he was under threat from actual or potential enemies.

Key question
What form did the early purges take?

Key figure

Nicolai Yezhov (1895–1940)
Known as the 'poisoned dwarf' because of his diminutive stature and vicious personality, he became head of the NKVD in 1937. He was himself tried and shot three years later.

Key terms

Ryutin group
Followers of M.N. Ryutin, a Right Communist, who had published an attack on Stalin, describing him as 'the evil genius who had brought the Revolution to the verge of destruction'.

Party card
The official CPSU document granting membership and guaranteeing privileges to the holder. It was a prized possession in Soviet Russia.

Paranoia
A persecution complex which gives the sufferer the conviction that he is surrounded by enemies intent on harming him.

Key dates

Beginning of the purges as a systematic terror system: 1934

Trial of the Ryutin group: 1932

Purges began under Yezhov: 1933

Legal system brought under Stalin's control: 1933–34

One historian, Alec Nove, offers this suggestion as to how Stalin's mind may have worked:

> The revolution from above caused great hardships, coercion left many wounds. Within and outside the Party, they might dream of revenge. Party leaders rendered politically impotent might seek to exploit the situation. So: liquidate them all in good time, destroy them and their reputations.

Robert Service writes that Stalin had 'a gross personality disorder' and adds:

> He had a Georgian sense of honour and revenge. Notions of getting even with adversaries never left him. He had a Bolshevik viewpoint on Revolution. Violence, dictatorship and terror were methods he and fellow party veterans took to be normal. The physical extermination of enemies was entirely acceptable to them.

Such thinking on Stalin's part meant that everyone was suspect and no one was safe. In Service's words, Stalin saw 'malevolent human agency in every personal or political problem he encountered'. Purges became not so much a series of episodes as a permanent condition of Soviet political life. Terror was all-pervading. Its intensity varied from time to time, but it was an ever-present reality throughout the remainder of Stalin's life.

Mechanisms of control

In the years 1933–34 Stalin centralised all the major law enforcement agencies:

- the civilian police
- the secret police
- labour camp commandants and guards
- border and security guards.

Key term

NKVD
The state secret police, a successor of the *Cheka* and a forerunner of the KGB.

All these bodies were put under the authority of the **NKVD**, a body which was directly answerable to Stalin. To tighten control even further, legal proceedings were also made subject to central control. In addition, a special military court, which stood outside the ordinary legal system, was created to deal with 'serious crimes', a term that was elastic enough to cover any offences which Stalin and his ministers considered threatening to their authority. For example 'counter-revolutionary activity' was designated a serious crime, but since the term was never precisely defined it could be applied to any misdemeanour no matter how trivial.

It was the existence of such a system that made the purges possible to operate on such a huge scale. The knowledge that anyone could be arrested at any time on the slightest of pretexts helped to maintain the atmosphere of terror and uncertainty that Stalin turned into a system of political and social control.

2 | The Post-Kirov Purges, 1934–36

Key question
In what ways did the post-Kirov purges tighten Stalin's control over the CPSU?

In Leningrad on 1 December 1934, a man named Leonid Nicolaev walked into the Communist Party headquarters and shot dead Sergei Kirov, the secretary of the Leningrad soviet. The apparent motive was revenge: Kirov had been having an affair with the killer's wife. But dramatic though the incident was in itself, its significance went far beyond the tale of a jealous husband. There is a strong probability that the murder of Kirov had been approved, if not planned, by Stalin himself. Nikita Khrushchev in his secret speech of 1956 (see page 128) stated that Stalin was almost certainly behind the murder. However, a special study concluded in 1993 that while Stalin may well have been guilty, the evidence against him consists of 'unverified facts, rumours and conjectures'.

Key dates

Assassination of Kirov: 1 December 1934

Intensification of the purges under Yagoda: 1934

Yezhov, Vyshinsky and Beria took over organising the purges: 1935

Whatever the truth concerning Stalin's involvement, it was certainly the case that the murder worked directly to his advantage. Kirov had been a highly popular figure in the Party. A strikingly handsome Russian, he had made a strong impression at the Seventeenth Party Congress in 1934 and had been elected to the Politburo. He was known to be unhappy with the speed and scale of Stalin's industrialisation drive. He was also opposed to extreme measures being used as a means of disciplining Party members. If organised opposition to Stalin were to form within the Party, Kirov was the outstanding individual around whom dissatisfied members might rally. That danger to Stalin had now been removed.

Stalin was quick to exploit the situation. Within two hours of learning of Kirov's murder he had signed a **Decree against Terrorist Acts** (also known as 1st December Decree). Under the guise of hunting down those involved in Kirov's murder, a fresh purge of the Party was begun. Stalin claimed that the assassination had been organised by a wide circle of Trotskyites and Leftists, who must all be brought to account. There followed a large-scale round-up of suspected conspirators, who were then imprisoned or executed.

Key term

Decree against Terrorist Acts (1st December Decree) This gave the NKVD limitless powers in pursuing enemies of the state and the Party.

The atmosphere was caught in an account by Victor Serge, one of the suspects who managed to flee from the USSR at this time:

> The shot fired by Nikolaev ushered in an era of panic and savagery. The immediate response was the execution of 114 people, then the execution of Nikolaev and his friends; then the arrest and imprisonment of the whole of the former Zinoviev and Kamenev tendency, close on 3,000 persons; then the mass deportation of tens of thousands of Leningrad citizens, simultaneously with hundreds of arrests among those already deported and the opening of fresh secret trials in the prisons.

Party membership

It was an interesting coincidence that just as Stalin's path to power had been smoothed 10 years earlier by 'the Lenin enrolment' (see page 16), so in 1934 his successful purge was made a great deal easier by a recent major shift in the make-up of the Party.

Key question
What was the relationship between the growth in Party membership and the purges?

Key figures

Gengrikh Yagoda (1891–1938)
Sadistic head of the NKVD, 1934–36; Stalin had him shot in 1938.

Andrei Zhdanov (1896–1948)
Dedicated follower of Stalin, described by one contemporary Communist as 'a toady without an idea in his head'.

Andrei Vyshinsky (1883–1954)
A reformed Menshevik, notorious for his brutal language and manner. He later served as Stalin's Foreign Secretary.

Lavrenti Beria (1899–1953)
A rapist, child molester and a repellent mixture of cruelty and cowardice, Beria rose to become Stalin's chief representative. He lost influence after Stalin's death and despite begging on his knees for his life, he was shot in 1956.

Alexander Poskrebyshev (1861–1965)
Personal secretary to Stalin for many years after 1929, he remained loyal to his master even though Stalin had his wife tortured and shot.

During the previous three years, in 'the Stalin enrolment', the CPSU had recruited a higher proportion of skilled workers and industrial managers than at any time since 1917. Stalin encouraged this as a means of tightening the links between the Party and those actually operating the First Five-Year Plan, but it also had the effect of bringing in a large number of members who joined the Party primarily to advance their careers. Acutely aware that they owed their privileged position directly to Stalin's patronage, the new members eagerly supported the elimination of the anti-Stalinist elements in the Party. After all, it improved their own chances of promotion. The competition for good jobs in Soviet Russia was invariably fierce. Purges always left positions to be filled. As the chief dispenser of positions, Stalin knew that the self-interest of these new Party members would keep them loyal to him. As Norman Stone, a Western analyst of the Soviet Union, memorably put it:

> It was characteristic of Stalin to have his own allies 'marked' by their own subordinates: in Stalin's system identical thugs kept on replacing each other, like so many Russian dolls.

The full-scale purge that followed Kirov's murder in 1934 was the work of **Gengrikh Yagoda**, head of the NKVD. In 1935 Kirov's key post as Party boss in Leningrad was filled by **Andrei Zhdanov**. The equivalent position in Moscow was filled by another ardent Stalinist, Nikita Khrushchev. In recognition of his strident courtroom bullying of 'oppositionists' in the earlier purge trials, **Andrei Vyshinsky** was appointed State Prosecutor.

Stalin's fellow Georgian, **Lavrenti Beria**, was entrusted with overseeing state security in the national-minority areas of the USSR. With another of Stalin's protégés, **Alexander Poskrebyshev**, in charge of the Secretariat, there was no significant area of the Soviet bureaucracy which Stalin did not control. Public or Party opinion meant nothing when set against Stalin's grip on the key personnel and functions in Party and government. There had been rumours, around the time of the Second FYP (see page 49), of a possible move to oust him from the position of Secretary General. These were silenced in the aftermath of the Kirov affair.

The outstanding feature of the post-Kirov purges was the status of many of the victims. Prominent among those arrested were Kamenev and Zinoviev, who, along with Stalin, had formed the triumvirate after Lenin's death in 1924 and who had been the leading Left Bolsheviks in the power struggle of the 1920s. At the time of their arrest in 1935 they were not accused of involvement in Kirov's assassination, only of having engaged in 'opposition', a charge that had no precise meaning and therefore could not be answered. However, the significance of their arrest and imprisonment was plain to all: no Party members, whatever their rank or revolutionary pedigree, were safe.

Arbitrary arrest and summary execution became the norm. In the post-Stalin years it was admitted by Khrushchev that the Decree against Terrorist Acts had become the justification for 'broad acts which contravened socialist justice', a euphemism for mass

murder. An impression of this can be gained from glancing at the
fate of the representatives at the Party Congress of 1934.

- Of the 1996 delegates who attended, 1108 were executed during
  the next three years.
- In addition, out of the 139 Central Committee members elected
  at that gathering all but 41 were put to death during the purges.

Leonard Shapiro, in his study of the CPSU, described these events
as 'Stalin's victory over the Party'. From this point on, the Soviet
Communist Party was entirely under his control. It ceased, in
effect, to have a separate existence. Stalin had become the Party.

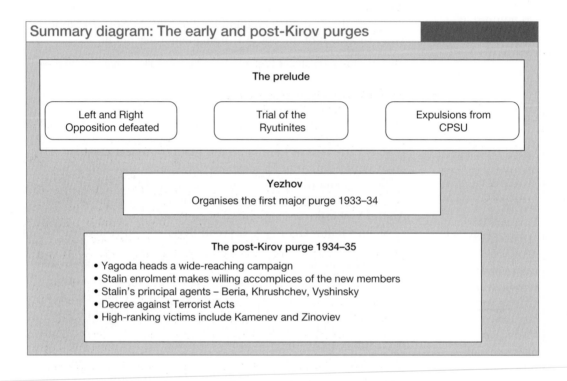

Summary diagram: The early and post-Kirov purges

The prelude

| Left and Right Opposition defeated | Trial of the Ryutinites | Expulsions from CPSU |

Yezhov
Organises the first major purge 1933–34

The post-Kirov purge 1934–35
- Yagoda heads a wide-reaching campaign
- Stalin enrolment makes willing accomplices of the new members
- Stalin's principal agents – Beria, Khrushchev, Vyshinsky
- Decree against Terrorist Acts
- High-ranking victims include Kamenev and Zinoviev

3 | The Great Purge, 1936–39

It might be expected that once Stalin's absolute supremacy over
the Party had been established the purges would stop. But they did
not; they increased in intensity. Stalin declared that the Soviet
Union was in 'a state of siege' and called for still greater vigilance
in unmasking the enemies within. In 1936 a progressive terrorising
of the Soviet Union began which affected the entire population,
but took its most dramatic form in the public show trials of Stalin's
former Bolshevik colleagues. The one-time heroes of the 1917
Revolution and the Civil War were arrested, tried and imprisoned
or executed as enemies of the state.

Remarkably, the great majority went to their death after
confessing their guilt and accepting the truth of the charges

Key question
Was there any logic
to the Great Purge?

**The Great Purge of
Party, Army and
people: 1936–39**

Key date

levelled against them. Such was the scale of the persecution at this time, and so high ranking were the victims, that it has gone down in history as 'the Great Purge' or 'the Great Terror'.

The descriptions applied to the accused during the purges bore little relation to political reality. 'Right', 'Left' and 'Centre' opposition blocs were identified and the groupings invariably had the catch-all term 'Trotskyite' tagged on to them, but such words were convenient prosecution labels rather than definitions of a genuine political opposition. They were intended to isolate those in the Communist Party and the Soviet state whom Stalin wished to destroy.

Stalin's terror programme breaks down conveniently into three sections:

a) The purge of the Party.
b) The purge of the armed services.
c) The purge of the people.

Key question
Why was there so little resistance from the Party members who were purged?

a) The purge of the Party
The purging of the Left
The prelude to the Great Purge of 1936 was a secret letter sent from CPSU headquarters, warning all the local Party branches of a terrorist conspiracy by 'the Trotskyite–Kamenevite–Zinovievite–Leftist Counter-Revolutionary Bloc' and instructing Party officials to begin rooting out suspected agents and sympathisers. Once this campaign of denunciation and expulsion had been set in motion in the country at large, Kamenev and Zinoviev were put on public trial in Moscow, charged with involvement in Kirov's murder and with plotting to overthrow the Soviet state. Both men pleaded guilty and read out abject confessions in court.

The obvious question is: 'Why did they confess?' After all, these men were tough Bolsheviks. No doubt, as was later revealed during de-Stalinisation, physical and mental torture was used. Possibly more important was their sense of demoralisation at having been accused and disgraced by the Party to which they had dedicated their lives and which could do no wrong. In a curious sense, their admission of guilt was a last act of loyalty to the Party.

Whatever their reasons, the fact that they did confess made it extremely difficult for other victims to plead their own innocence. If the great ones of state and Party were prepared to accept their fate, on what grounds could lesser men resist? The psychological impact of the public confessions of such figures as Kamenev and Zinoviev was profound. It helped to create an atmosphere in which innocent victims submitted in open court to false charges, and went to their death begging the Party's forgiveness.

It also shows Stalin's astuteness in insisting on a policy of public trials. There is little doubt that he had the power to conduct the purges without using legal proceedings. He could simply have had the victims bumped off. However, by making the victims deliver humiliating confessions in open court, Stalin was able to reveal the scale of the conspiracy against him and to prove the need for the purging to continue.

The purging of the Right

This soon became evident after Kamenev and Zinoviev, along with 14 other Bolsheviks, had been duly executed in keeping with Vyshinsky's notorious demand as Prosecutor that they be shot 'like the mad dogs they are'. The details that the condemned had revealed in their confessions were used to prepare the next major strike, the attack upon 'the Right deviationists'. Bukharin, Rykov and Tomsky were put under investigation, but not yet formally charged. The delay was caused by the reluctance of some of the older Bolsheviks in the Politburo to denounce their comrades. Stalin intervened personally to speed up the process. Yagoda, who was considered to have been too lenient in his recent handling of the 'Trotskyite–Zinovievite bloc', was replaced as head of the NKVD by the less scrupulous Yezhov whose name, like Vyshinsky's, was to become a byword for terror.

The 'anti-Soviet Trotskyist Centre'

Meanwhile, the case for proceeding against Bukharin and the Right was strengthened by the revelations at a further show trial in 1937, at which 17 Communists, denounced collectively as the 'anti-Soviet Trotskyist Centre', were charged with spying for Nazi Germany. The accused included **Karl Radek** and **Georgy Pyatakov**, the former favourites of Lenin, and **Grigory Sokolnikov**, Stalin's Commissar for Finance during the First Five-Year Plan. Radek's grovelling confession in which he incriminated his close colleagues, including his friend Bukharin, saved him from the death sentence imposed on all but three of the other defendants. He died two years later, however, in an Arctic labour camp.

Yezhov and Vyshinsky now had the evidence they needed. In 1938, in the third of the major show trials, Bukharin and Rykov (Tomsky had taken his own life in the meantime) and 18 other 'Trotskyite–Rightists' were publicly arraigned on a variety of counts, including sabotage, spying and conspiracy to murder Stalin. The fact that Yagoda was one of the accused was a sign of the speed with which the terror was starting to consume its own kind. **Fitzroy MacLean**, a British diplomat, was one of the foreign observers permitted to attend the trial. His description conveys the character of the proceedings:

> The prisoners were charged, collectively and individually, with every conceivable crime: high treason, murder, and sabotage. They had plotted to wreck industry and agriculture, to assassinate Stalin, to dismember the Soviet Union for the benefit of their capitalist allies. They were shown for the most part to have been traitors to the Soviet cause ever since the Revolution. One after another, using the same words, they admitted their guilt: Bukharin, Rykov, Yagoda. Each prisoner incriminated his fellows and was in turn incriminated by them.

Key figures

Karl Radek (1885–1939)
A leading Bolshevik propagandist since 1905, he had been head of the Comintern in the early 1920s.

Georgy Pyatakov (1890–1937)
An economist who held a number of important government posts in the 1920s and 1930s.

Grigory Sokolnikov (1888–1939)
A finance minister under both Lenin and Stalin.

Fitzroy MacLean (1911–96)
A young Scottish diplomat and adventurer who took a keen personal interest in the purges.

At one point in the trial Bukharin embarrassed the court by attempting to defend himself, but he was eventually silenced by Vyshinsky's bullying and was sentenced to be shot along with the rest of the defendants. In his final speech in court, Bukharin showed the extraordinary character of the Bolshevik mentality. Despite the injustice of the proceedings to which he had been subjected, he accepted the infallibility of the Party and of Stalin:

> When you ask yourself: 'If you must die, what are you dying for?' – an absolutely black vacuity suddenly rises before you. There was nothing to die for, if one wanted to die unrepented. And, on the contrary, everything positive that glistens in the Soviet Union acquires new dimensions in a man's mind. This in the end disarmed me completely and led me to bend my knees before the Party and the country ... For in reality the whole country stands behind Stalin; he is the hope of the world.

The Stalin Constitution, 1936

A particular irony attached to Bukharin's execution. Only two years previously he had been the principal draftsman of the new constitution of the USSR. This 1936 Constitution, which Stalin described as 'the most democratic in the world', was intended to impress Western Communists and Soviet sympathisers. This was the period in Soviet foreign policy when, in an effort to offset the Nazi menace to the USSR, Stalin was urging the formation of 'popular fronts' between the Communist parties and the various left-wing groups in Europe. Among the things claimed in the Constitution were that:

- Socialism having been established, there were no longer any 'classes' in Soviet society.
- The basic civil rights of freedom of expression, assembly and worship were guaranteed.

However, the true character of Stalin's Constitution lay not in what it said but in what it omitted. Hardly anywhere was the role of the Party mentioned; its powers were not defined and, therefore, were not restricted. It would remain the instrument through which Stalin would exercise his total control of the USSR. The contrast between the Constitution's democratic claims and the reality of the situation in the Soviet Union could not have been greater.

Lenin's General Staff of ᴸᴼᴵᴵ

STALIN, THE EXECUTIONER, ALONE REMAINS

RYKOV	BUKHARIN	SVERDLOV	STALIN	ZINOVIEV	KAMENEV	TROTSKY	LENIN
Shot	Shot	Dead	Survivor	Shot	Shot	In Exile	Dead

KOLLONTAI	URITSKY	KRESTINSKY	SMILGA	NOGIN	DZERZHINSKY	BUBNOV	SOKOLNIKOV
Missing?	Dead	Shot	Shot	Dead	Dead	Disappeared	In Prison

LOMOV	SHOMYAN	BERZIN	MURANOV	ARTEM	STASSOVA	MILIUTIN	JOFFE
?	Dead	?	Disappeared	Dead	Disappeared	Missing	Suicide

The Central Committee of The Bolshevik Party in 1917

This montage, composed by Trotsky's supporters, points to the remarkable fact that of the original 1917 Central Committee of the Bolshevik Party only Stalin was still alive in 1938. The majority of the other 23 members had, of course, been destroyed in the purges.

b) The purge of the armed services

A significant development in the purges occurred in 1937 when the Soviet military came under threat. Stalin's control of the Soviet Union would not have been complete if the armed services had continued as an independent force. It was essential that they be kept subservient. Knowing that military loyalties might make a purge of the army difficult to achieve, Stalin took the preliminary step of organising a large number of transfers within the higher ranks in order to lessen the possibility of centres of resistance being formed when the attack came.

With this accomplished, Vyshinsky announced, in May 1937, that 'a gigantic conspiracy' had been uncovered in the Red Army. **Marshal Mikhail Tukhachevsky**, the popular and talented Chief of General Staff, was arrested along with seven other generals, all of whom had been 'heroes of the Civil War'. On the grounds that speed was essential to prevent a military coup, the trial was held immediately, this time in secret. The charge was treason; Tukhachevsky was accused of having spied for Germany and Japan. Documentary evidence, some of it supplied by German intelligence at the request of the NKVD, was produced in proof.

The outcome was predetermined and inevitable. In June 1937, after their ritual confession and condemnation, Tukhachevsky and his fellow generals were shot. There appears to have been a particularly personal element in all this. The president of the secret court which delivered the death sentences was **Marshal Klimenty Voroshilov**, a devoted Stalinist who had long been jealous of Tukhachevsky's talent and popularity.

Key question
Why did Stalin regard the leaders of the Soviet armed services as a threat to his power?

Key figures

Marshal Mikhail Tukhachevsky (1893–1937)
A founder of the Red Army under Lenin and Trotsky.

Marshal Klimenty Voroshilov (1881–1969)
One of the founding members of the Bolshevik Party, he became a devoted Stalinist.

Tukhachevsky's execution was the signal for an even greater blood-letting. To prevent any chance of a military reaction, a wholesale destruction of the Red Army establishment was undertaken. In the following 18 months:

- All 11 War Commissars were removed from office.
- Three of the five Marshals of the Soviet Union were dismissed.
- 91 of the 101-man Supreme Military Council were arrested, of whom 80 were executed.
- 14 of the 16 army commanders, and nearly two-thirds of the 280 divisional commanders, were removed.
- Half of the commissioned officer corps, 35,000 in total, were either imprisoned or shot.

At the height of the purge extraordinary scenes were witnessed in some army camps where whole lorry loads of officers were taken away for execution. The Soviet Navy did not escape the purges: between 1937 and 1939 all the serving admirals of the fleet were shot and thousands of naval officers were sent to labour camps. The Soviet Air Force was similarly decimated during that period, only one of its senior commanders surviving the purge.

The devastation of the Soviet armed forces, wholly unrelated to any conceivable military purpose, was complete by 1939. It left all three services seriously undermanned and staffed by inexperienced or incompetent replacements. Given the defence needs of the USSR, a theme constantly stressed by Stalin himself, the deliberate crippling of the Soviet military is the aspect of the purges that most defies logic. It suggests that Stalin had lost touch with reality.

c) The purge of the people

Key question
Why did the purges continue?

Stalin's achievement of total dominance over Party, government and military did not mean the end of the purges. The apparatus of terror was retained and the search for enemies continued. Purges were used to achieve the goals of the FYPs: charges of industrial sabotage were made against managers and workers in the factories. The purge was also a way of forcing the regions and nationalities into total subordination to Stalin.

The show trials that had taken place in Moscow and Leningrad, with their catalogue of accusations, confessions and death sentences, were repeated in all the republics of the USSR. The terror they created was no less intense for being localised. For example, between 1937 and 1939 in Stalin's home state of Georgia:

- two state prime ministers were removed
- four-fifths of the regional Party secretaries were removed from office
- thousands of lesser officials lost their posts.

Key figure

**Béla Kun
(1886–1938)**
Leader of the short-lived Communist government in Hungary in 1938.

This was accompanied by a wide-ranging purge of the legal and academic professions. Foreign Communists living in the Soviet Union were not immune. Polish and German revolutionary exiles were rounded up in scores, many of them being subsequently imprisoned or executed. The outstanding foreign victim was **Béla Kun**, who was condemned and shot in 1938.

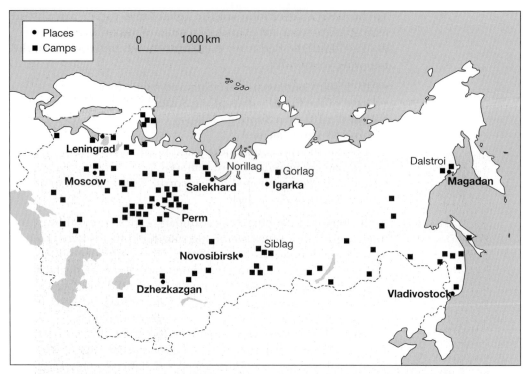

Figure 4.1: The Soviet labour camps, 1937–57. By 1941, as a result of the purges, there were an estimated eight million prisoners in the *gulag*. The average sentence was ten years, which, given the terrible conditions in the camps, was equivalent to a death sentence. As an example of state-organised terror, Stalin's *gulag* stands alongside Hitler's concentration camps and Mao Zedong's laogai (Chinese prison camp system) in its attempt to suppress the human spirit.

Mass repression

Understandably, historians have tended to concentrate on the central and dramatic features of the purges, such as the show trials and the attack upon the Party and the Red Army. Yet no area of Soviet life entirely escaped the purges. Under Stalin, terror was elevated into a method of government. The constant fear that this created conditioned the way the Soviet people lived their lives. European scholars who have been working since the early 1990s in the newly opened archives in the former Soviet Union have discovered that, in terms of numbers, the greatest impact of the purges was on the middle and lower ranks of Soviet society.

- One person in every eight of the population was arrested during Stalin's purges.
- Almost every family in the USSR suffered the loss of at least one of its members as a victim of the terror.

This was not an accidental outcome of the purges. The evidence now shows that in the years 1937–38 Yezhov deliberately followed a policy of mass repression. This '**Yezhovschina**' involved NKVD squads going into a range of selected localities, then arresting and dragging off hundreds of inhabitants to be executed. The killings

Key terms

Gulag
The vast system of prison and labour camps that spread across the USSR during the purges.

Yezhovschina
The period of terror directed at ordinary Soviet citizens in 1937–38 and presided over by Yezhov, the head of the NKVD.

Key date

The Yezhovschina persecutions in the localities: 1937–38

were carried out in specially prepared NKVD zones. One notorious example of this was Butovo, a village some 15 miles south of Moscow, which became one of the NKVD's killing grounds. Recent excavations by the Russian authorities have revealed mass graves there containing over 20,000 bodies, dating back to the late 1930s. Forensic analysis of the bodies, which were found piled on top of each other in rows, indicates that nightly over many months victims had been taken to Butovo and shot in batches of a hundred.

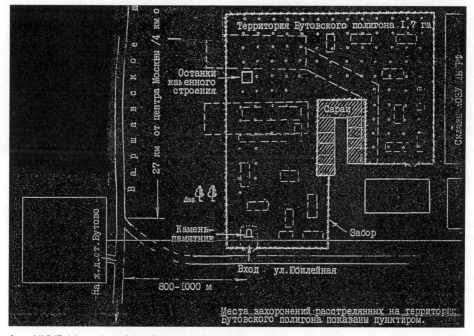

Part of an NKVD blueprint of the Butovo killing fields. The cross-hatched area shows the pit into which the victims were heaped after being shot.

The quota system

The number of victims to be arrested was laid down in set quotas as if they were industrial production targets. People were no longer regarded as individuals. It was the numbers not the names that mattered. There was no appeal against sentence and the death warrant invariably required that the execution 'be carried out immediately'.

One incident illustrates the mechanical, dehumanised process. A woman whose neighbour had been arrested called at a police station to ask permission to look after the child the neighbour had had to leave behind. After leaving her waiting for two hours, the police then decided that since they were one short of their daily quota of people to be arrested the caller would make up the number. She was grabbed and thrown into a cell.

Insofar as the terrorising of ordinary people had a specific purpose, it was to frighten the USSR's national minorities into abandoning any lingering thoughts of challenging Moscow's control and to force waverers into a full acceptance of Stalin's enforced industrialisation programme.

Stalin signing an order for the execution of 6600 condemned prisoners. An interesting point of comparison is that this number exceeded that of all those executed for political offences in tsarist Russia in the 100 years up to 1917.

The purges go full circle

In the headlong rush to uncover further conspiracies, interrogators themselves became victims and joined those they had condemned in execution cells and labour camps. Concepts such as innocence and guilt lost all meaning during the purges. The mass of the population were frightened and bewildered. Fear had the effect of destroying moral values and traditional loyalties. The one aim became survival, even at the cost of betrayal. In a 1988 edition devoted to the Stalinist purges, the Moscow *Literary Gazette* referred to 'the special sadism whereby the nearest relatives were forced to incriminate each other – brother to slander brother, husband to blacken wife'. The chillingly systematic character of the purges was described in the minutes of a plenary session of the Central Committee, held in June 1957 during the **de-Stalinisation** period.

> Between 27 February 1937 and 12 November 1938 the NKVD received approval from Stalin, Molotov and Kagonovich for the Supreme Court to sentence to death by shooting 38,697. On one day, 12 November 1938, Stalin and Molotov sanctioned the execution of 3,167 people. On 21 November the NKVD received approval from Stalin and Molotov to shoot 229 people, including twenty-three members and candidate members of the Central Committee, twenty-two members of the Party Control Commission, twelve regional Party secretaries, twenty-one People's Commissars, 136 commissariat officials and fifteen military personnel.

De-Stalinisation
The movement, begun by Khrushchev in 1956, to expose Stalin's crimes and mistakes.

Key term

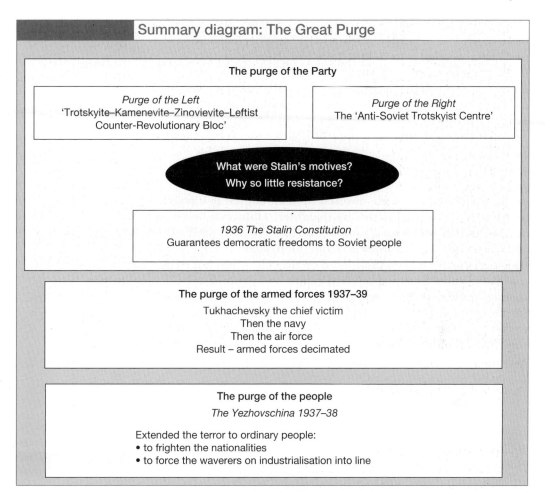

Summary diagram: The Great Purge

The purge of the Party

Purge of the Left
'Trotskyite–Kamenevite–Zinovievite–Leftist Counter-Revolutionary Bloc'

Purge of the Right
The 'Anti-Soviet Trotskyist Centre'

What were Stalin's motives?
Why so little resistance?

1936 The Stalin Constitution
Guarantees democratic freedoms to Soviet people

The purge of the armed forces 1937–39
Tukhachevsky the chief victim
Then the navy
Then the air force
Result – armed forces decimated

The purge of the people
The Yezhovschina 1937–38

Extended the terror to ordinary people:
• to frighten the nationalities
• to force the waverers on industrialisation into line

Key question
Why did the Stalinist purges continue into the war and the post-war period?

4 | The Later Purges, 1941–53

The purges did not end with the onset of war in 1941 or with the coming of peace in 1945. They had become an integral part of the Stalinist system of government. Stalin blamed military failures on internal sabotage and persecuted those held responsible. Nor did victory soften him. He emerged from the war harder in attitude towards the Soviet people, despite their heroic efforts, and more suspicious of the outside world, despite the alliances entered into by the USSR. It was undeniable that many Soviet troops had deserted to the enemy in the early phases of the war. When peace came, Stalin used this to justify a large-scale purge of the Soviet armed forces.

Key dates

Purges removed those accused of undermining the war effort: 1941–45

Purging of Soviet people believed to have supported Germany: 1945

'The Leningrad Affair'

As he grew older Stalin became still more suspicious of those around him. After 1947 he dispensed with the Central Committee and the Politburo, thus removing even the semblance of a restriction on his authority. In 1949 he initiated another Party purge, 'the Leningrad Affair', comparable in scale and style to those of the 1930s. Leading Party and city officials, including those who had previously been awarded the title 'Hero of the Soviet Union' in honour of their courageous defence of Leningrad during the war, were arrested, tried on charges of attempting to use Leningrad as an opposition base, and shot.

Key dates

The Leningrad Affair: 1949

The Doctors' Plot: 1953

Stalin died: March 1953

The 'Doctors' Plot'

Soviet Jews were the next section of the population to be selected for organised persecution. Anti-Semitism was a long-established tradition in Russia and it was a factor in the last purge Stalin attempted. He ordered what amounted to a **pogrom** for no better reason than that his daughter, Alliluyeva, had had an affair with a Jewish man of whom he disapproved. Early in 1953 it was officially announced from the **Kremlin** that a 'Doctors' Plot' had been uncovered in Moscow; it was asserted that the Jewish-dominated medical centre had planned to murder Stalin and the other Soviet leaders. Preparations began for a major assault on the Soviet medical profession, comparable to the pre-war devastation of the Red Army. What prevented those preparations being put into operation was the death of Stalin in March 1953.

Key terms

Pogrom
State-organised persecution involving physical attacks upon Jews and the destruction of their property.

Kremlin
The former tsarist fortress in Moscow that became the centre of Soviet government.

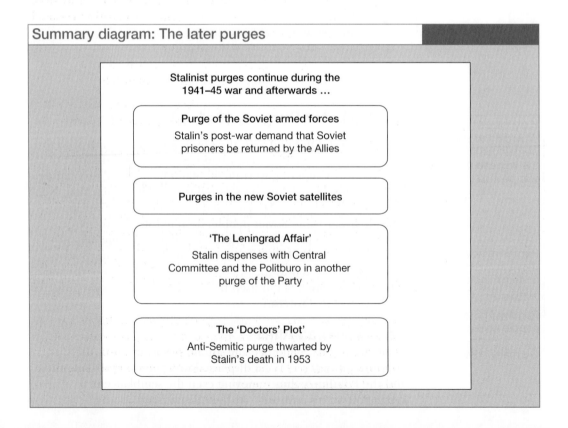

Summary diagram: The later purges

Stalinist purges continue during the 1941–45 war and afterwards …

Purge of the Soviet armed forces
Stalin's post-war demand that Soviet prisoners be returned by the Allies

Purges in the new Soviet satellites

'The Leningrad Affair'
Stalin dispenses with Central Committee and the Politburo in another purge of the Party

The 'Doctors' Plot'
Anti-Semitic purge thwarted by Stalin's death in 1953

Key question
Why did Stalin persist with such a destructive policy from 1933 to his death?

5 | The Purges as a Study in Stalin's Use of Power

Stalin's use of terror as a political and social weapon is a grim but fascinating theme. It is still not possible for historians to give a precise figure of those destroyed during the purges. However, in the 1990s, access to the files of the KGB was granted to scholars. Major studies, such as Anne Applebaum's *The Gulag* (2003), which complements the earlier pioneering study by Robert Conquest, *The Great Terror* (see page 54), enable us to quote the following figures as the most reliable now available:

- In 1934, one million people were arrested and executed in the first major purge, mainly in Moscow and Leningrad.
- By 1937, seven to eight million had been transported to labour camps; four million of these died.
- By 1939, another five to seven million had been 'repressed', one million of these being shot, another one to two million dying in the camps.
- In 1940, the occupation of the Baltic states (Lithuania, Estonia and Latvia), Bukovina and Bessarabia resulted in two million being deported, most of whom died.
- In 1941, the deportation to Siberia of various national groups, including Germans, Kalmyks, Ukrainians, Chechens and Crimean Tatars, led to the deaths of one-third of the four million involved.
- Between 1944 and 1946, the 'screening' of returned prisoners of war and those who had been under German occupation resulted in 10 million being transported to labour camps of the gulag; five to six million of these died in captivity.
- Between 1947 and 1953, one million died in the various purges and repressions during the last six years of Stalin's life.

It is disturbing to reflect that, in the sheer scale of its misery and death, the Stalinist repression of the Soviet peoples far exceeded even the Nazi **holocaust**.

Only a partial answer can be offered as to why Stalin engaged for so long in such a brutal exercise. One motive was obviously the desire to impose his absolute authority by bringing all the organs of Party and state under his control. Yet, even after that aim had been achieved, the terror continued. The purges were so excessive and gratuitously vicious that they make logical analysis difficult. Stalin destroyed people not for what they had done but for what they might do. His suspicions and fears revealed a deeply distorted mind. That, indeed, was how Stalin's daughter, Svetlana Alliluyeva, explained his irrationality:

Key term

Holocaust
The genocide of six million Jews in occupied Europe between 1939 and 1945.

> As he'd got older my father had begun feeling lonely. He was so isolated from everyone that he seemed to be living in a vacuum. He hadn't a soul he could talk to. It was the system of which he himself was the prisoner and in which he was stifling from emptiness and lack of human companionship.

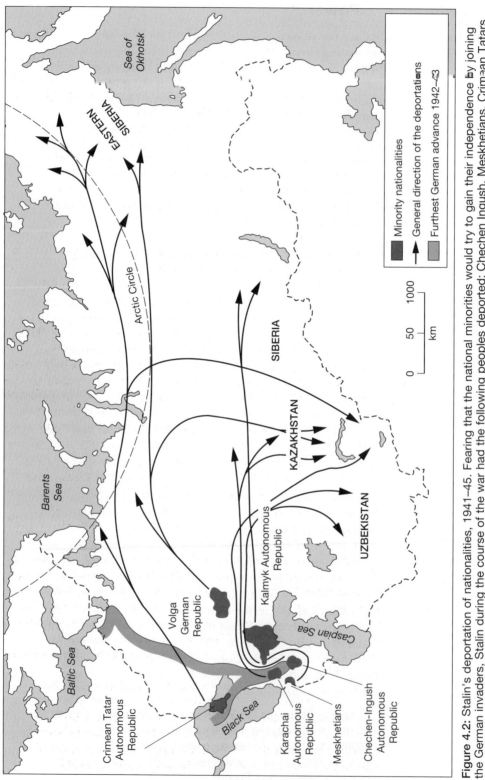

Figure 4.2: Stalin's deportation of nationalities, 1941–45. Fearing that the national minorities would try to gain their independence by joining the German invaders, Stalin during the course of the war had the following peoples deported: Chechen Ingush, Meskhetians, Crimean Tatars, Kalmyks, Karachai, and Volga Germans. The brutality with which the deportations were enforced caused great suffering and many thousands died. In all, it is reckoned that by 1945 some 20 million Soviet people had been uprooted.

6 | The Key Debate

> How far beyond Stalin did the responsibility for the purges and the terror spread?

Robert Service, one of the most celebrated biographers of Stalin, says of him: 'Nowadays, virtually all writers accept that he initiated the Great Terror.' Yet Service, along with all the leading experts in the field, is careful to acknowledge that, while Stalin was undoubtedly the architect of the terror, the responsibility for implementing it goes beyond Stalin. Prompted by their reading of Russian archival material that has become available, historians suggest that Stalinism was not as monolithic a system of government as has been traditionally assumed. Attention has shifted to the disorganised state of much of Soviet bureaucracy, particularly at local level.

The character of Soviet politics and society

Key question
Was Soviet Communism intrinsically violent?

The purges were clearly initiated by Stalin himself, but he, after all, was only one man, no matter how powerful or feared. How the purges were actually carried out largely depended on the local party organisation. Many welcomed the purges as an opportunity to settle old scores as well as a way of advancing themselves by filling the jobs vacated by the victims. It has to be acknowledged that the purges were popular with some Russians – those who believed their country could be prevented from slipping back into its historic weakness and backwardness only by being powerfully and ruthlessly led. To such people, Stalin was a genuine saviour whose unrelenting methods were precisely what the nation needed.

It is also arguable that the disruption of Soviet society, caused by the massive upheavals of collectivisation and industrialisation, destroyed any semblance of social cohesion and so encouraged Party and government officials to resort to the most extreme measures. Civil society as it existed in Russia was not strong enough or advanced enough to offer an alternative to what was being done in the name of the Communist Revolution.

Richard Overy, a distinguished expert on modern European history, draws attention to the violence that he regards as having been intrinsic in Soviet Communism. He quotes Stalin's assertion that 'the law of violent proletarian revolution is an inevitable law of the revolutionary movement' and links it directly with Lenin's declaration that the task of Bolshevism was 'the ruthless destruction of the enemy'. The Stalinist purges, therefore, were a logical historical progression.

In this connection, other scholars have laid weight on how undeveloped the concepts of individual or civil rights were in Russia. Tsardom had been an autocracy in which the first duty of the people had been to obey. Lenin and the Bolsheviks had not changed that. Indeed, they had re-emphasised the necessity of obedience to central authority. The purges were a deadly extension of that principle.

An interesting interpretation relating to the idea that violence was an irremovable feature of Russian Communism has been advanced by a number of modern scholars, among whom J. Arch Getty is the most prominent. Their suggestion is that the purges came from below as much as from above. They mean by this that the purges begun by Stalin were sustained in their ferocity by the lower rank officials in government and Party who wanted to replace their superiors, whom they regarded as a conservative elite. This elite would never give up its power willingly so it had to be smashed. Russian political tradition did not allow any alternative.

The nomenklatura

It was certainly true Stalin had no difficulty in finding eager subordinates to organise the purges. The common characteristic of those who led Stalin's campaigns was their unswerving personal loyalty to him, a loyalty that overcame any doubts they might have had regarding the nature of their work. They formed what became known as the **nomenklatura**, the new class of officials whom Stalin created to replace the thousands of old Bolsheviks whom he eliminated in the purges.

One prominent historian, M. Agursky, has stressed this development as a major explanation of why terror became so embedded in the Stalinist system. The nomenklatura had no loyalty to the old Bolshevik tradition. They were all totally Stalin's men:

> To replace the old elite there came a new stratum which had no continuity with its predecessors for the purges took place in different phases and in the end liquidated the entire body of activists who had taken part in the Revolution and the Civil War.

Dedicated to Stalin, on whom their positions depended, the nomenklatura enjoyed rights and privileges denied to the rest of the population. Including their families, they numbered by the late 1930s an exclusive group of only 600,000 out of a population of 150 million. It was what came with the job that mattered: members had plentiful food rations, luxury accommodation, motor cars, specially reserved Party lanes for them to drive on, and top quality education for their children (see page 114). Once in post, persons with such privileges were unlikely to risk them by questioning Stalin's orders. The more potential rivals they exterminated, the safer their jobs were.

Geoffrey Hosking, a major scholar of Russian history, has also described how the purges provided opportunities for the new type of Communist Party official: 'Local party bosses, naturally enough, exploited the purge to bolster their own patronage, advance their own clients, and get rid of their opponents.' Hosking makes the additional point that Stalin's realisation of how self-centred Party officials were intensified his determination not to lose control over them. That was the reason for both his maintenance of the terror and for the willingness of his underlings to be the eager practitioners of terror.

Key term

Nomenklatura
The Soviet 'establishment' – a privileged elite of officials who ran the Party machine.

The role of ideology and idealism

In a major study, *Stalin: The Court of the Red Tsar* (2003), Simon Sebag Montefiore has illustrated the eagerness with which Stalin's top ministers carried out his campaigns of terror and persecution. Though they were terrified of him, they did not obey him simply out of fear. People like Yezhov, Beria and Molotov derived the same vindictive satisfaction from their work as their master. Like him, they appeared to have no moral scruples. Sebag Montefiore describes the extraordinary mixture of fear and callousness that made up the lives of the people Stalin surrounded himself with in the Kremlin under his tsar-like rule:

> Stalin was utterly unique but many of his views and features such as dependence on death as a political tool, and his paranoia, were shared by his comrades. They lived on ice, killing others to stay alive, sleeping with pistols under their pillows, their wives murdered on Stalin's whim, their children living by a code of lies. Yet they kept their **quasi-religious faith** in the Bolshevism that justified so much death.

In reviewing Sebag Montefiore's book, David Satter, himself an authority on Stalin's Russia, adds the following insight into how and why the purges operated as they did:

> The Stalinist enterprise consisted of the effort to remake the social system of a vast country on the basis of a **utopian** ideology. In carrying out this task, Stalin and his henchmen in many ways resembled powerful bureaucrats anywhere, but these were bureaucrats freed of all moral restraints. Their duties as functionaries explained why the members of Stalin's court not only enthusiastically fulfilled execution quotas but insisted on over-fulfilling them.

A further insight into the Soviet mind-set that permitted all this to happen is offered by the Russian historian Dimitri Volkogonov, a biographer of Stalin:

> People like Stalin regard conscience as a **chimera**. One cannot speak of the conscience of a dictator; he simply did not have one. The people who did his dirty deeds for him, however, knew full well what they were doing. In such people conscience had 'gone cold'. In consequence, the people allowed their own consciences to be driven into a reservation, thus giving the grand inquisitor the authority to carry on with his dark deeds.

Yet when seeking to explain the motives of those who implemented the vast terror that overtook the Soviet Union, one should not leave out the role of idealism. It may now be judged a perverted idealism but it was compelling enough to those who shared it to convince them that the arrests, the shootings, and the gulag were all justified since they were leading ultimately to the triumph of the Revolution and the creation of a Communist paradise on earth.

Key terms

Quasi-religious faith
A conviction so powerful that it has the intensity of religious belief.

Utopian
Belief in the attainability of a perfect society.

Chimera
A powerful but ultimately meaningless myth.

Some key books in the debate:
M. Agursky, *Stalin's Background* (*Survey* No. 4, 1984)
Svetlana Alliluyeva, *Twenty Letters to a Friend* (Penguin, 1968)
Anne Applebaum, *Gulag: A History of the Soviet Camps* (Penguin, 2003)
J. Arch Getty and R.T. Manning, *Stalinist Terror: New Perspectives* (Cambridge, 1993)
Robert Conquest, *The Great Terror: Stalin's Purge of the Thirties* (Penguin, 1971)
Geoffrey Hosking, *Russia and the Russians* (Allen Lane, 2001)
Alec Nove, *Stalinism and After* (Unwin Hyman, 1975)
Richard Overy, *The Dictators: Hitler's Germany and Stalin's Russia* (Allen Lane, 2004)
Donald Rayfield, *Stalin and His Hangmen: The Tyrant and Those who Killed for Him* (Random House, 2003)
Simon Sebag Montefiore, *Stalin: The Court of the Red Tsar* (Knopf, 2003)
Robert Service, *Stalin: A Biography* (Macmillan, 2004)
Robert C. Tucker, *Stalinism – Essays in Historical Interpretation* (Transaction Publishers, 1999)
Lynne Viola, *The Unknown* Gulag: *The Lost World of Stalin's Special Settlements* (OUP, 2007)
Dmitri Volkogonov, *Stalin: Triumph and Tragedy* (Weidenfeld and Nicolson, 1991)

Study Guide: AS Questions

In the style of AQA

(a) Explain why Stalin signed the Decree against Terrorist Acts in December 1934. (12 marks)

(b) 'The purges and the Great Terror between 1934 and 1941 strengthened Stalin's position considerably.' Explain why you agree or disagree with this view. (24 marks)

Exam tips

(a) Any answer to this question will need to explain the immediate context – the assassination of Kirov, the apparent danger to the Communist Party and the need to find those involved in Kirov's murder. However, a good answer will also include the broader motivation – Stalin's desire for personal control, his concern for security, undisputed leadership and the need to purge the Party of any who might challenge his power. Stalin's paranoia about 'Trotskyites' and supporters of the Left were certainly reasons for the decree and possibly he was already growing worried about others within the Communist ranks. Try to link your factors in a sensible way to indicate the most important or over-riding reasons.

(b) The quotation in question (b) is deliberately provocative. You will be aware from reading this chapter that the purges and Great Terror actually weakened the USSR in many respects, so whether you choose to agree or disagree with the quotation you will need to balance the positive and negative results. For Stalin, of course, the purges and Great Terror meant the elimination of enemies and political rivals as well as the firm establishment of personal control through fear. It enabled him to press forward with his plans for industrialisation and collectivisation and it reinforced his cult of personality, adding to ideas of infallibility. It forced the regions into obedience and subdued the nationalities. However, the loss of personnel in the armed forces left them undermanned and inadequately led, the legal and academic professions were decimated and, even in politics, the purges ensured there was no successor being trained and the brightest individuals who might have helped the country in its drive to modernisation had been removed. Experts disappeared from many spheres, including industry, while in the country as a whole, obedience through 'fear' rather than support might be said to be a weakness for Stalin's leadership. Whatever your argument, try to provide a balanced analysis and supported judgement.

In the style of Edexcel

How far do Stalin's fears and suspicions account for the extent of the terror in the USSR in the years 1936–39? (30 marks)

Exam tips

The cross-references are intended to take you straight to the material that will help you to answer the question.

The question is not simply asking you to explain why there was a terror in the USSR. Every word in an examination question has been put there for a purpose. Notice here the question is about the 'extent' of the terror. So, even if you feel there is no doubt that Stalin was responsible for the purges, were other factors involved in accounting for the sheer scale of them?

Notice, too, the question asks you about the importance of Stalin's fears and suspicions. Did he have other reasons for implementing the purges which arose not from fear, but from other motives?

Remember, too, that simply telling the examiner how extensive and terrifying the purges were will earn you few marks. The question wants an explanation for, not a description of, the terror.

Below is a collection of material that will help you formulate your argument. You should aim to organise your information into three areas:

- Evidence that Stalin's fears and suspicions were key.
- Evidence that Stalin had additional motives.
- Evidence that other factors also played a part.

You should only use the information about the nature and extent of the purges to illustrate these factors.

Evidence that Stalin's fears and suspicions were key
- Stalin's wish to impose absolute authority (pages 60, 62, 75)
- Stalin's wish to force regions and nationalities into subordination (pages 69, 71)
- Stalin's fear of what people might do in the future (page 61)

Evidence that Stalin had additional motives
- Purge of the Party (pages 65–66)
- Purge of the armed services (pages 68–69)
- Mass repression (pages 70–71)

Evidence that other factors also played a part
- The role of local Party organisation (pages 63–64)
- The ferocity of the purges generated from below (page 77)
- Communism as an intrinsically violent movement (pages 77–78)
- The motives and actions of the nomenklatura (pages 78–79)
- The role of ideas and attitudes within the USSR (pages 70–72, 75)

And what is your overall conclusion? How much was due to Stalin's fears and suspicions?

5 The Great Patriotic War, 1941–45

POINTS TO CONSIDER
Between 1941 and 1945 Stalin's Russia was put to its greatest test in the most murderous war of the twentieth century. From the verge of utter defeat in 1941, it recovered to win a total triumph over Hitler's armies in 1945. How the Soviet Union came to be involved in war in 1941 and its experience in the titanic struggle that ensued are examined under the following themes:

- The road to war
- The Soviet Union at war, 1941–45.

Key dates

1933–39	Nazi Germany a constant threat to Soviet security
1934	USSR admitted to the League of Nations
1936	Anti-Comintern Pact signed by Germany, Italy and Japan
1938	Munich Agreement appeared to isolate USSR
1939	Nazi–Soviet Pact between Germany and USSR
	Soviet–German agreement to divide Poland
1941	Hitler unleashed Operation Barbarossa against Soviet Union
1941–45	The Great Patriotic War
1942–43	Battle of Stalingrad
1943	Battle of Kursk
1945	Yalta (February) and Potsdam (July) Conferences

Key figure

Marshal Georgi Zhukov (1896–1974) Chief of the Soviet General Staff in June 1941, he became the great Soviet military hero of the 1941–45 war.

At 3.40 a.m. on 22 June 1941, Stalin received a shattering phone call. It was from **Marshal Georgi Zhukov**, who told him that a three million-strong German army had just launched Operation Barbarossa, a massive invasion of the western USSR. The future of the nation was now at hazard. To understand how Stalin and the Soviet Union came to be in such a perilous position, we need to examine the key aspects of Stalin's foreign policy which culminated in the dramatic events of June 1941.

1 | The Road to War

Lenin's legacy in foreign affairs

The Revolution of 1917 had left Soviet Russia as the only Communist nation in a hostile world. Knowing that the USSR was relatively weak militarily when compared with the Western nations, Lenin had feared that those states would 'gang up' to attack the Soviet Union. To delay, if not prevent, that occurring Lenin had adopted an essentially defensive position. In 1921 he had declared, 'Our foreign policy while we are alone and while the capitalist world is strong consists in our exploiting contradictions.' What he meant was that Soviet Russia would protect itself not by provoking the capitalist nations but by playing on the differences that separated them from each other. The conflicting self-interest of such countries as France, Britain and Germany would be exploited by the Soviet Union to prevent the build-up of an anti-Communist alliance.

As a result, it was compromise rather than confrontation that was the guiding principle of the foreign policy that Stalin inherited from Lenin. He continued it by adopting the same defensive attitude towards the outside world. There is, therefore, an important distinction to be made between the theory and the practice of Soviet foreign policy under Stalin:

- Judged by its propaganda, the USSR under Stalin was pledged to the active encouragement of worldwide revolution. The Comintern existed for this very purpose.
- However, in practice, Stalin did not regard Soviet Russia as being strong enough to sustain a genuinely revolutionary foreign policy. As he saw it, his overriding duty was not to pursue international revolution but to work to ensure the survival of the Soviet Union by following a policy that involved the lowest risk to the nation.
- This attitude was an aspect of his 'Socialism in One Country', putting the needs of the USSR above all other considerations (see page 25). Stalin did not want military conflict with the powerful nations of Western Europe. Wherever possible he avoided confrontation abroad.

The German threat

Stalin's conciliatory approach was particularly evident in regard to Germany. Initially, he sought to develop good Soviet–German relations by encouraging mutual trade agreements between the two countries and by giving little real support to the German Communist Party. However, once **Adolf Hitler** came to power in Germany in 1933 it became impossible for Stalin to maintain such a policy. Hitler's hatred of Communism was of the same rabid quality as his anti-Semitism. Throughout the 1930s, Nazi Germany conducted a vicious propaganda campaign against the Soviet Union as an evil Marxist state.

This, together with violent Nazi attacks upon the German Communist Party and open discussion among German diplomats of their country's ultimate aim of expanding into the USSR,

Key question
How committed was Stalin to international revolution?

Key figure

Adolf Hitler (1889–1945)
Leader of the National Socialist German Workers' Party and dictator of Germany 1933–45.

Key date

Nazi Germany a constant threat to Soviet security: 1933–39

Key terms

League of Nations
The body set up in 1919 with the aim of resolving all international disputes and so maintaining world peace.

Collective security
Nations acting together to protect individual states from attack.

Anti-Comintern Pact
Formed by the fascist nations, Germany, Italy and Japan, it carried a clear threat of a two-front attack on the Soviet Union's European and Far Eastern borders.

Versailles Settlement
The peace treaty of 1919 which redrew the map of Europe.

convinced Stalin that Hitler's Germany was a menace that had somehow to be nullified. After 1933 it was no longer possible to pursue a pro-German policy.

For the next six years Stalin tried to offset the German danger by finding allies in Western Europe. One of the earliest opportunities for him to lessen the isolation of the USSR came with its admission into the **League of Nations** in 1934. The League provided a platform for the Soviet Union to call for the adoption of the principle of **collective security** in international affairs. One of the fruits of this was an agreement in 1935 between the USSR, France and Czechoslovakia, promising 'mutual assistance' if one of the partners suffered military attack.

However, such gains as the new approach in Soviet foreign policy achieved proved largely superficial. Collective security was impressive as a principle, but did not work in practice in the 1930s. The basic weakness was that Europe's two most powerful states, France and Britain, were not prepared to risk war in order to uphold the principle. Without their participation, there was no possibility of collective security becoming a reality.

The threat to the USSR intensifies, 1936–39
The Anti-Comintern Pact
The year 1936 proved to be particularly bleak for the USSR's hopes of sheltering under collective security. Late in that year the **Anti-Comintern Pact** was formed, aimed directly against the Soviet Union. The danger that this represented threatened to destroy all the efforts made by the Soviet Union to establish its security. It led Stalin to redouble his efforts to obtain reliable allies and guarantees. However, in his attempts to achieve this, Stalin was labouring under a handicap, largely of his own making. The plain fact was that Soviet Russia was not trusted. Enough was known of the Stalinist purges to make neutrals in other countries wary of making alliances with a nation where such treachery or tyranny was possible.

The Munich Agreement

Key dates

USSR joined League of Nations: 1934

Formation of the Anti-Comintern Pact: November 1936

The Munich Agreement: 1938

In the autumn of 1938, France, Britain, Italy and Germany signed the Munich Agreement, the climax to the Czech crisis. This arose from Hitler's demand that the Sudetenland, an area which in 1919 had been incorporated into Czechoslovakia, be allowed to become part of Germany. He had threatened invasion if his requirements were not met. Although Hitler's demand was in breach of the **Versailles Settlement**, neither Britain nor France was prepared to resist him militarily. The Munich Agreement granted all his major demands.

'WHAT, NO CHAIR FOR ME?'

Low's cartoon of September 1938 accurately captured Stalin's response to the Munich settlement, which formally accepted Germany's demand for possession of the Sudeten region of Czechoslovakia. The Russian leader viewed the Munich conference, to which the USSR had pointedly not been invited despite its formal alliance of 1935 with Czechoslovakia, as a Western conspiracy. The other people represented are Hitler, Neville Chamberlain, Daladier of France, and Mussolini.

In the Western world, the Munich settlement has customarily been seen as an act of 'appeasement', part of the Anglo-French policy of avoiding war by making concessions to the aggressor, Germany. That was not the interpretation put upon it by Stalin. For him, Munich was a gathering of the anti-Soviet nations of Europe, intent on giving Germany a free hand to attack a diplomatically isolated USSR. Stalin declared that 'a new imperialist war' was inevitable. **Maxim Litvinov** spoke for him when he said at the time of Munich: 'International relations are entering an era of the most violent upsurge of savagery and brute force and the policy of the mailed fist.'

Desperate now to achieve some form of security, if only temporarily, Stalin redoubled his efforts to reach agreement with France and Britain. In the year after Munich, Litvinov and his successor as foreign secretary, Molotov, delivered a series of formal alliance proposals to the French and British governments. These went unanswered. France and Britain could not bring themselves to trust Stalin. This left him with only one course of action. If he could not form an alliance *against* Germany, he would have to form an alliance *with* Germany. That is what he instructed his foreign office officials and diplomats to work to achieve.

The Nazi–Soviet Pact

The successful climax to their efforts came in August 1939 when the seemingly impossible happened. Two deadly international enemies, Hitler's Germany and Stalin's Russia, came together in a formal agreement. Molotov, the new Soviet foreign minister, and

Key question
How did Stalin view the Munich Agreement?

Maxim Litvinov (1876–1951)
The USSR's foreign secretary from 1930 to May 1939.

Key figure

Key question
Why was the Soviet Union willing to sign a non-aggression pact with Nazi Germany in 1939?

his German counterpart, Ribbentrop, signed the Nazi–Soviet Pact, in which both countries gave a solemn pledge to maintain peaceful relations with each other. The key articles read:

> Article I. The Government of the German Reich and the Government of the USSR obligate themselves to desist from any act of violence, any aggressive action, and any attack on each other, either individually or jointly with other powers.

> Article VI. The present treaty is concluded for a period of ten years.

In a 'Secret Additional Protocol', it was agreed that the USSR would take over the **Baltic States** and that Poland would later be divided between Germany and the USSR. At the beginning of September 1939, German forces began to occupy Poland. Four weeks later, under the terms of the protocol, Germany and the Soviet Union signed a formal agreement which effectively carved up Poland between them.

The Nazi–Soviet Pact bewildered the USSR's friends and puzzled its foes. It seemed to defy history and logic. An official at the British Foreign Office dryly remarked that with the coming together of fascism and Communism, Nazism and Marxism, 'all these -isms are now -wasms'. But there was a rationale to this remarkable change in Soviet foreign policy. Given the real threat that Germany presented and the indifference of Paris and London to his offers of a defensive alliance, Stalin felt he had been left no alternative. He had acted on the axiom 'If you can't beat them, join them', and had attempted to end the danger from Germany by the only move that international circumstances still allowed – an agreement with Germany.

The fruits of the Pact were gathered by both countries during the next two years. The USSR duly grabbed the eastern half of Poland.

Key term

Baltic States
Estonia, Latvia and Lithuania.

Key dates

Signing of the Nazi–Soviet Pact: August 1939

Soviet–German agreement to divide Poland: 28 September 1939

Molotov signs the Nazi–Soviet Pact on 23 August 1939. A smiling Stalin looks on.

Germany was free to conduct its war against France and Britain in the west, while in the east the USSR added to its Polish prize by forcibly taking hold of the Baltic States, southern Finland, and Bessarabia-Bukovina. By 1941 Soviet Russia had regained all the territories it had lost as a result of the First World War. All this, added to the guarantee of peace with Germany, seemed to justify the praise heaped on Stalin inside the Soviet Union for his diplomatic master-stroke.

The extravagant claim made for the Nazi–Soviet Pact was that it had safeguarded Soviet security by a guarantee of freedom from Western attack, and had thus fulfilled the chief objective for which Soviet foreign policy had been struggling since the days of Lenin. It is one of the inexplicable things about Stalin that he remained oblivious to the fact that Hitler's ultimate aim in foreign affairs was the invasion and occupation of Russia. An outstanding and consistent feature of Nazism from its beginnings had been its conviction that Germany's destiny was to expand eastwards at the expense of the Slav lands, including Russia. That was the one clear strategy to be deduced from Hitler's **Mein Kampf**.

After August 1939, Stalin chose to ignore all this. It is remarkable that he failed to realise that the Pact, which gave Germany a free hand in the war which broke out in Western Europe in September 1939, made the German invasion of Russia likely to come sooner rather than later. He was thus unready for the German attack when it was launched in June 1941.

Mein Kampf
'My Struggle', the title of Hitler's autobiographical book, written in the 1920s and regarded as the Nazi bible.

Key term

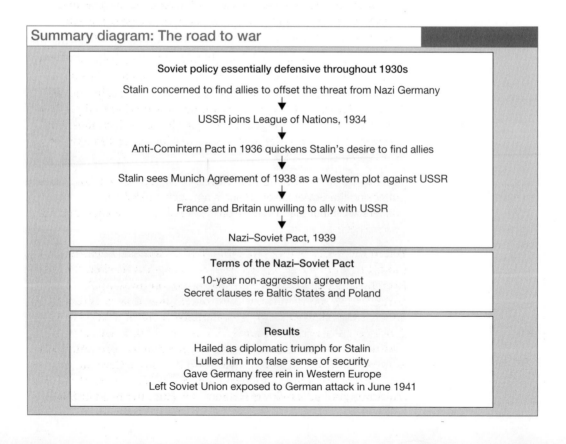

Summary diagram: The road to war

Soviet policy essentially defensive throughout 1930s

Stalin concerned to find allies to offset the threat from Nazi Germany
↓
USSR joins League of Nations, 1934
↓
Anti-Comintern Pact in 1936 quickens Stalin's desire to find allies
↓
Stalin sees Munich Agreement of 1938 as a Western plot against USSR
↓
France and Britain unwilling to ally with USSR
↓
Nazi–Soviet Pact, 1939

Terms of the Nazi–Soviet Pact
10-year non-aggression agreement
Secret clauses re Baltic States and Poland

Results
Hailed as diplomatic triumph for Stalin
Lulled him into false sense of security
Gave Germany free rein in Western Europe
Left Soviet Union exposed to German attack in June 1941

2 | The Soviet Union at War, 1941–45

The German invasion, 1941

Key question
Why was Stalin so badly caught out by the German invasion of the Soviet Union?

The war which began in Europe in 1939 went very well for Germany for the first two years. France and the Low Countries were overrun in 1940, Italy joined the war as a German ally, and, although Britain held on, it seemed only a matter of time before she, too, would be defeated. These remarkable successes encouraged Hitler to launch his long-intended attack upon the USSR on 22 June 1941. Operation Barbarossa, Hitler's own code-name for the invasion, was on such a huge scale that preparations for it could not be concealed. In the preceding months millions of German troops had been moved into the frontier areas.

Key date
Operation Barbarossa launched: 22 June 1941

Stalin's attitude

Stalin did not dispute that the German forces were being deployed in great numbers. What he could not bring himself to believe was that all this activity presaged an actual invasion. He told his officials that it was British counter-intelligence which was distorting the picture of German manoeuvres to make them seem more sinister than they were. The British plan was to panic the Soviet Union into precipitate action against Germany. That was why Stalin refused to allow the Soviet forces to respond in any way that the Germans could regard as provocative. In an address to his military commanders in May 1941 Stalin told them:

> You must understand that Germany will never on its own move to attack Russia. If you provoke the Germans on the border, if you move forces without our permission, then bear in mind heads will roll.

His conviction was that Hitler would not risk a two-front war. Until Britain had been defeated and the war fully concluded in the west, Germany would not move against Russia. In May, Stalin said to Zhukov, 'Hitler and his generals are not so stupid as to fight at the same time on two fronts.' A month later he was still certain that he had assessed the situation correctly, asserting on 11 June, only 11 days before the attack:

> I am certain that Hitler will not risk creating a second front by attacking the Soviet Union. Hitler is not such an idiot and understands that the Soviet Union is not Poland, not France, and not even England.

Key figures

Richard Sorge (1895–1944)
Codenamed 'Ramsay', the Soviet Union's most celebrated and most successful spy.

Pavel Fitin (1907–71)
Became chief of the NKVD's foreign intelligence service in 1939.

Yet, in the weeks before Operation Barbarossa was unleashed, a mounting number of reports from Soviet agents reached the Kremlin warning that Germany was intent on invasion. A particularly striking warning came on 15 June, a week before the attack, from **Richard Sorge**, a Comintern agent in Japan. He provided hard evidence that Germany was about to launch a massive assault on western Russia. When Stalin was presented with Sorge's report he wrote dismissively on it: 'This is German disinformation.' On the following day Stalin received further news confirming Sorge's story, this time from **Fitin**, the head of Soviet security. Fitin informed Stalin that a reliable source in the **Luftwaffe** had warned, 'Preparations for an armed invasion of the USSR are fully complete and the attack may be expected at any time.' Stalin's reaction was to write angrily to Fitin's boss, **Merkulov**, the Minister for State Security: 'You can tell your "source" in German air force headquarters to go fuck himself. He's not a "source", he's a disinformer.'

Vsevolod Merkulov (1895–1953)
MInister of State Secrutiy of the USSR in 1941.

Key figure

Explanations for Stalin's attitude

With hindsight, Stalin's refusal to acknowledge the imminent German invasion and to prepare against it appears inexplicable. Yet in a fascinating study, *Fateful Choices* (Penguin, 2007), the eminent British historian, Ian Kershaw, has pointed out how limited Stalin's options were in 1941. The Soviet army was simply not strong enough to make a pre-emptive strike against Germany. All the Soviet Union could do in such circumstances was to maintain the line of least resistance, hoping that German aggression would be deterred. This explains why right down to the eve of the June invasion it continued to offer more and more military and economic concessions to Germany. Even as the German troops crossed the Soviet borders on 22 June, lorries and railway wagons were being loaded with materials to be sent to Germany under the terms of the various Soviet–German trade agreements.

Key question
Was there any logic to Stalin's refusal to accept the threat of invasion?

There is also the consideration that Stalin was a victim of his own propaganda. He could not bring himself to admit that the Nazi–Soviet Pact, which had for two years been portrayed to the Soviet people as an example of his matchless statesmanship, had failed. Perhaps he genuinely believed that he could use the terms of the Pact to divert or buy off Hitler.

Yet whatever the puzzles attaching to Stalin's inaction, its consequences were abundantly clear. Because he was unwilling to admit the reality of the situation in June 1941, none of his underlings could take the initiative. For two days after the German invasion had started, Stalin remained in his **dacha** outside Moscow, saying little and giving no instructions. The result was that in the first week of the Second World War, on the eastern front, the German forces overran a Soviet Union that was without effective leadership or direction.

Luftwaffe
The German air force.

Dacha
Country villa.

Key terms

Stalin's greatest mistake was not in misreading German intentions in 1941 but in having decimated his armed services in the purge of 1938–39 (see page 68). It was this that left the Soviet army so ill-prepared to face the greatest invasion in Russian history. And yet it remains undeniable that having brought the Soviet Union to the brink of defeat, Stalin stayed to lead it to recovery and victory. It is unlikely that without Stalin's leadership the USSR could have survived its great ordeal. Ian Kershaw has drawn attention to the admission made by Marshal Zhukov after the war that, had Stalin accepted the plan put forward by some of his generals for a pre-emptive strike to start in May, then all the probabilities were that the Soviet forces would have been smashed beyond recovery and the USSR defeated in 1941.

Hitler declared that the world would hold its breath when it witnessed Operation Barbarossa. He had every right to be dramatic. It was a huge enterprise, unprecedented in the history of warfare. Germany put into the field:

- three million troops
- half a million motorised vehicles
- 4000 tanks
- 3000 aircraft.

Yet this great array was more than equalled by the Soviet Union which had the larger forces:

- It matched Germany in the number of troops.
- It had four times the number of tanks.
- It had three times the number of aircraft.

However, it would take time for the Soviet Union to gather and deploy these forces; in the interim the initiative lay with the invading armies.

The failure of the German forces to take the USSR

Despite the deadly German onslaught which it suffered, the USSR remained undefeated by the beginning of 1942, the time by which Hitler had calculated on total victory for his armies. Four key factors explain the Soviet survival:

- Stalin's recovery of nerve
- the lateness of the launching of Barbarossa
- **'General Winter'**
- Nazi racism.

Key term

'General Winter'
A popular way by which Russians traditionally referred to the many occasions when their country had been saved from an aggressor by the onset of bitter winter conditions.

Stalin's recovery of nerve

Stalin had been overcome by a deep despondency in the early days of the German invasion. On one of the very rare occasions when he expressed a sense of guilt, he had remarked, 'Lenin left us a great legacy and we have fucked it up.' Yet once he had thrown off his depression he began to show the strength of leadership for which he became renowned for the rest of the war. He showed total commitment to the task of leading his country's fight for survival. In his first radio broadcast of the war on 3 July 1941, he appealed to the people to defend 'Mother Russia' by adopting the scorched-earth methods of warfare that had always saved the nation in its glorious past:

> The issue is one of life and death for the peoples of the USSR. We must mobilise ourselves and reorganise all our work on a new wartime footing, where there can be no mercy to the enemy. In areas occupied by the enemy, sabotage groups must be organised to combat enemy units, to foment guerrilla warfare everywhere, to blow up bridges and roads, damage telephone and telegraph lines, to set fire to forests, stores and transports. In occupied regions, conditions must be made unbearable for the enemy.

The same sense of desperate defiance prompted Stalin's resolve
not to leave Moscow in October 1941 when the city seemed about
to fall to the Germans. His determination to stay, despite the
urging of many of his ministers who wanted him to go, had an
inspiring effect. Accepting the word of Marshal Zhukov that
Moscow could be held, Stalin chose to remain. His gesture lifted
the morale of the Soviet army and people. Molotov later said that
had Stalin left at that critical stage, 'Moscow would have burned
and the Soviet Union would have collapsed.'

The lateness of the launching of Barbarossa
Events elsewhere in Europe had delayed the start of Hitler's
Russian campaign by some six weeks from its originally planned
date. This meant that, in spite of the rapid and crushing advance
of German forces, the expected Russian capitulation had not come
by the autumn of 1941. Neither Moscow nor Leningrad, though
heavily besieged by then, had fallen.

'General Winter', 1941–42
The thick mud of a torrential autumn was followed by the snow
and ice of one the severest winters in Russian memory. German
movement slowed to a dead halt. Russian forces were able to
regroup and begin a counter-attack under Marshal Zhukov in
December 1941. Germany was now involved in a struggle on its
eastern front that would decide the outcome of the war itself.

Nazi racism
Spirited though Soviet resistance ultimately proved to be, it is
significant that in the early stages of the German invasion
opposition was far from total. Indeed, one of the most remarkable
aspects of the Barbarossa campaign was that in many areas along the
front, the local Soviet population at first welcomed the invaders.
Some were even willing to join the German forces. This was not
from love of Germany but from hatred of Stalinism. Had the
German high command grasped the significance of this they might
have enlisted the people of the occupied areas in a great anti-Stalin
crusade. A top German official, **Otto Brautigam**, described how,
when first entering the Soviet Union, 'we found on our arrival a
population weary of Bolshevism. The population greeted us with joy
as liberators and placed themselves at our disposal.'

However, blinded by Nazi racial theory, the Germans treated
the areas they overran with calculated savagery. The consequence,
in Brautigam's words, was that:

> our policy has forced both Bolsheviks and Russian nationalists into a
> common front against us. The Russian fights today with exceptional
> bravery and self-sacrifice for nothing more or less than recognition of
> his human dignity.

Germany was eventually to pay a terrible price for this. The Soviet
people responded to German brutality by committing themselves
to a desperate struggle for survival which earned itself the title, the

Key figure

Otto Brautigam
(1900–48)
Deputy leader of
the German
Ministry for the
Occupied East.

Key date

The Great Patriotic War (also known as the Great Fatherland War): 1941–45

Key question

Why was the war on the eastern front so bitter and destructive?

Key terms

War of attrition
A grinding conflict in which each side hopes to win by wearing the other down.

Normandy landings
The Allied opening of a second front in Europe by a large-scale American–British invasion in western France.

Geneva Convention
International agreements in 1906 and 1929 which had laid down the humane ways in which POWs should be treated.

Great Patriotic War, which climaxed in victory in 1945. In pushing into eastern Germany in the closing stages of the war, the Red Army subjected the civilian population to the same ferocity which the Soviet people had suffered.

The character of the war, 1941–45

The early initiative lay with the German invader. But the longer the war went on, the greater the opportunities became for the Soviet Union not merely to avoid defeat but to triumph over the German forces. The USSR's struggle against Germany was a simple one in its essentials. It was a **war of attrition**. From near-defeat in 1941 the Soviet Union drew the German forces deeper and deeper into Russia until they were overstretched and vulnerable. The Soviet armies then counter-attacked, pushing the enemy back into Germany until Berlin itself fell in May 1945.

Soviet casualties were prodigious. In the worst years, 1941–42, the Red Army lost an average of 15,000 men each day. To put that in perspective: in one week its losses of over 100,000 matched that of all the British troops killed between the **Normandy landings** in June 1944 and the end of the war in May 1945. In the course of the war overall, more than five and a quarter million Soviet troops became prisoners of war. Four million of these POWs were shot or died in captivity. Since the USSR had not signed the **Geneva Convention**, Soviet prisoners had no protection, though it is doubtful, given the savagery with which the war was fought on the eastern front, whether either side would have honoured the Convention.

Nor was it merely a matter of death at the hands of the Germans. Despite the public accolades heaped upon the gallant soldiers in the official Soviet press and in Stalin's radio broadcasts, the Soviet leader and his military high command treated their troops with indifference or deliberate brutality. The following extract from a battle order indicates how terror was used as a standard method of motivating the Soviet forces:

1. Commanders and workers who during a battle desert or surrender to the enemy are to be considered malicious deserters. Their families are to be arrested as the relatives of deserters who have broken their oaths of service and betrayed their motherland. All commanders and commissars are to shoot deserters on the spot.

2. Units and sub-units that are surrounded by the enemy are to fight selflessly to the last man.

One of the cruellest aspects of Stalin's policy was any Soviet soldier who fell into German hands, far from being regarded with sympathy by Stalin, was deemed to be a traitor.

Two particular battles illustrate the character of the Soviet resistance and explain Germany's eventual defeat.

The Battle of Stalingrad

As part of their push south-eastward to seize the oil fields of the Caucasus, the German forces besieged the city of Stalingrad. The city was not of major strategic value, but it bore Stalin's name. Defining it as a symbol of Russian resistance, Stalin demanded that his city be defended to the death. Hitler's response was perfectly matched. It was recorded in the official high command report: 'The Führer orders that on entry into the city the entire male population be done away with.'

But having entered Stalingrad the Germans met such a ferocious resistance that they were forced onto the defensive. The besiegers became the besieged. Ignoring the appeals of his generals at the front, who urged a withdrawal, Hitler instructed his army to retreat not one millimetre. They were 'to fight to the last soldier and the last bullet'. The result was that the German forces, deprived of supplies and reinforcements, were battered and starved into submission. Their surrender on 31 January 1943 was a blow from which Germany never recovered.

- 200,000 German troops died in the battle.
- Another 91,000 became prisoners at its end; of these, only 6000 would survive their captivity.
- Hitler's Sixth Army, which had been the most successful of all Germany's forces since the start of the war, had been destroyed.

The Soviet forces themselves had suffered terribly. In the battle which occupied the winter months of 1942–43, over a million Soviet troops were killed. The life expectancy of a soldier at the front was 24 hours. Yet Stalingrad was singly the most important conflict of the war in Europe. It proved that Hitler's armies were not invincible and gave real promise of final victory to the Western allies. The Soviet newspaper, *Red Star*, summed up the significance of it all:

> What was destroyed at Stalingrad was the flower of the German Wehrmacht [army]. Hitler was particularly proud of the 6th Army and its great striking power. It was the first to invade Belgium. It took Paris. It took part in the invasion of Yugoslavia and Greece. In 1942 it broke through from Karkov to Stalingrad. And now it does not exist.

Key date

Battle of Stalingrad saw the deaths of over one million Soviet troops and 200,000 German soldiers: 1942–43

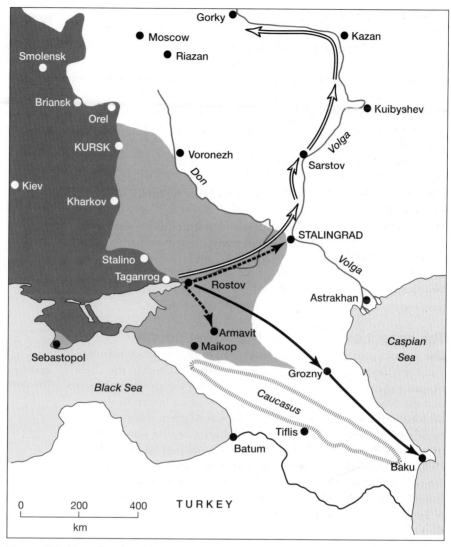

Figure 5.1: Map showing the position of Stalingrad and Kursk. Arrowed lines show the intended German offensives.

Key terms

Panzer
Fast armoured tank units.

Operation Citadel
The German code name for the Kursk campaign.

Salient
An area that protrudes into the enemy's lines forming a bulge.

The Battle of Kursk

It was in an effort to regain his army's prestige that Hitler backed a plan by his generals, who had noted that a large 'bulge' had appeared in the region of Kursk, where the Soviet forces had overextended their defensive line. If the Germans were to launch a full-scale **panzer** attack they could break through the Soviet line and so regain the initiative on the eastern front.

So it was that on 5 July 1943 **Operation Citadel** was begun. It produced the largest tank battle in history. The Soviet commanders with astonishing speed poured their forces into the Kursk **salient**. The number of troops and armaments deployed are shown in Table 5.1 on the following page.

Table 5.1: Troops and armaments used in the Battle of Kursk

	Troops	Tanks	Aircraft
German	700,000	2400	1800
Soviet	1,300,000	3400	2100

Battle of Kursk: July 1943

Key date

It was superior numbers that mattered. After 12 days of savage attack and counter-attack, the German forces still had not broken through. Mindful of Stalingrad, Hitler decided to save his armies from another devastating defeat by calling off the whole operation. The Soviet Union justifiably hailed it as another great victory. Kursk had confirmed what Stalingrad had first revealed: the Soviet forces were winning the war.

And so it proved. Over the next two years the Soviet army went on to the offensive. **Operation Bagration** in Belorussia in the summer of 1944 saw the defeat of the 1.2 million-strong German Army Group Centre, and opened the way for the Soviet forces to invade Germany itself and head for Berlin. In the spring of 1945, a battered, occupied, devastated Germany surrendered.

Operation Bagration (22 June–19 August 1944) The 58-day battle cost a combined total of 765,000 casualties.

Urals The mountain range dividing European Russia from its Asian east.

Key terms

The impact of the war on the Soviet people

The ferocity and scale of the four-year fight to the death meant that everything in the Soviet Union was subordinated to the sheer necessity of survival. Stalin's insistence during the previous 13 years that the Soviet economy be put on a war footing began to show obvious benefits. Centralised authority was of great value when it came to organising the war effort. Furthermore, the harshness of the conditions under which the Soviet people had laboured in the 1930s had prepared them for the fearful hardships of war. The raw courage and resilience of the Russian people, seemingly inured to suffering, proved a priceless asset.

← **Key question** How did the Soviet economy respond to the demands of war?

How much the Soviet people suffered can be expressed very simply. At the end of 1941, after only six months of war, the following losses had been suffered:

- half the Soviet population was under German occupation
- a third of the nation's industrial plant was in German hands
- iron and steel production had dropped by 60 per cent
- forty per cent of the railway system was no longer usable
- livestock had been reduced by 60 per cent
- grain stocks had been reduced by 40 per cent.

Wartime reorganisation

The reason for this early catastrophe was that under the Five-Year Plans Soviet industrial expansion had been sited west of the **Urals**, the area most vulnerable to German attack. To offset the losses, extraordinary efforts were then made to transfer whole sectors of Soviet industry to the relative safety of eastern USSR. Between July and December 1941, 2593 separate industrial enterprises were moved to the east, transported in 1.5 million railway freight cars.

All adults not involved in essential war work were conscripted into the armed forces. By 1944 there were over two million women serving in the Red Army. In a small touch of chivalry amidst the carnage and suffering, the government made the soap ration for female soldiers 100 grams more than for the men. Special all-female units were sometimes formed. One remarkable example was the 46th Guards Night Bomber Regiment, which the Germans nicknamed 'the night witches', a reference to the women pilots' tactic of switching off their engines as they attacked so that they glided in undetected by the enemy air defence crews. They made 'a whooshing sound, like a witch's broom stick in the night'.

The drafting of so many of the civilian population into the armed services, together with the huge number of casualties, amounting to four million in the first year of the war, meant that children, women and the elderly had to fill the vacant places in the factories. Work on the land similarly became an almost totally female activity. Arms production received top priority. By 1942 over half of the national income was being devoted to military expenditure. This was the highest proportion by far of any of the countries involved in the Second World War. In such circumstances the pre-war levels of production could not be maintained. Figure 5.2 indicates the degree of industrial disruption in the Soviet Union caused by the German occupation during the first two years of the war.

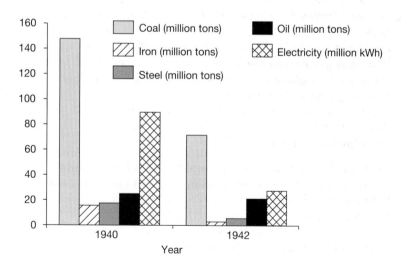

Figure 5.2: Industrial production in the USSR.

Key term

Lend-lease programme
The importing by the Soviet Union of war materials from the USA with no obligation to pay for them until after the war, an extension of the system by which earlier in the war the USA had provided aid to Britain.

The lowest point in Soviet economic fortunes came in 1942. But from then on, as things began to improve on the military front, there was a corresponding improvement in the economy. The new factories in the Urals began to come into production. The 17 million tons of war materials sent by the USA to the USSR under a **lend-lease programme** bolstered the Soviet's home-produced supply of weapons and motor transport. Of special significance was the recovery and expansion of the Soviet railway system, which enabled troops and supplies to be moved strategically. With the retreat of the German armies on a broad front, following their defeats in 1943 at Stalingrad and Kursk, the USSR began to regain its lost industrial sites. The scale of economic recovery that followed can be seen in Table 5.2.

Table 5.2: Wartime productivity in the USSR (calculated to a base unit of 100 in 1940)

	1941	1942	1943	1944
National income	92	66	74	88
Total industrial output	98	77	90	104
Armaments production	140	186	224	251
Fuel production	94	53	59	75
Agricultural output	42	38	37	54

These figures indicate the impressive response of the Soviet Union to the demands of war. The ability to achieve a huge arms production at a time of acute shortages in plant, materials and manpower is the outstanding example of this response.

The suffering of the Soviet people in wartime

However, the recovery was achieved at the expense of even greater privation for the Soviet people than they had already borne during collectivisation and industrialisation. The suffering was caused by the following factors:

- the long German occupation of the most fertile land
- the shortage of agricultural labour
- the reimposition of state grain and livestock requisitions
- the breakdown of the food distribution system.

All these combined to transform the chronic Russian food shortage into famine. Over a quarter of the estimated 25 million fatalities suffered by the Soviet Union during the war were the result of starvation. A fearful example of what was endured is evident in the statistics relating to the siege of Leningrad.

- The siege lasted 900 days from September 1941 to January 1944.
- A million people, one in three of the city's population, died from wounds, hunger or cold.
- Over 100,000 German bombs fell on the city.
- Over 200,000 shells were fired into the city.
- The police arrested 226 people for cannibalism, a token gesture at controlling what became a widespread practice.

As the Soviet military struggle drew to its successful close in May 1945, Stalin declared: 'We have survived the hardest of all wars ever experienced in the history of our Motherland. The point is that the Soviet social system has proved to be more capable of life and more stable than a non-Soviet system.' He chose not to admit that much of the suffering had been caused by his own policies, not least his mania for deporting whole peoples whose loyalty he doubted. It was an extension of the purges on a massive scale.

Stalin's treatment of returning Soviet POWs

In spite of his personal triumph, Stalin was, if anything, more paranoid at the end of the war than at the beginning. His suspicions of real or imagined enemies had grown, not weakened. The tragedy was that he was helped in this by the Western Allies. At the **Yalta and Potsdam Conferences** in 1945, the victor nations had agreed in principle that all released prisoners of war should be returned to their country of origin. In central and eastern Europe these included many Soviet citizens who had fought for Germany against the USSR in an attempt to break free of Stalin. They were terrified at the prospect of what awaited them and pleaded with their Allied captors not to be sent back. However, in the face of Stalin's insistence, the Allies gave in and forcibly repatriated the prisoners they held. There were heart-rending scenes as British troops forced Soviet prisoners at rifle and bayonet point to board the waiting trucks.

The consequences were as appalling as the prisoners had anticipated. Mass executions took place on Stalin's orders. What deepened the horror was that the victims were not only fighting-men. On the grounds that whole communities had supported Hitler's forces, whole communities were made to suffer. It was at this time that the Cossacks as a people were virtually destroyed in retribution for their support of the German armies during the war.

Stalin was no gentler on the Soviet POWs who returned from German captivity. Believing that their very survival indicated that they had collaborated with their captors, he treated them with contempt. It was not uncommon in 1945 for prisoners to be released from German prison camps, only to be transferred directly into Soviet labour camps.

Stalin as war hero

In the USSR at the end of the war, Stalin gave instructions that his role in the nation's military triumph be given the highest place. Paintings portraying him as the great war leader planning the victory of the Soviet Union adorned all public buildings. But Stalin had been no Hitler. Although he had been brutally unforgiving of those in the military he regarded as failures, he had had the good sense to allow his generals, such as Marshal Zhukov, real freedom to direct the war. At the great victory parade held in Moscow's Red Square in 1945 it was Zhukov, mounted on a white charger, who reviewed the troops. He made an impressive figure. Watching from the balcony above, Stalin became deeply jealous; he had originally intended to take the review himself but had changed his mind out of fear that he would not be able to control the horse.

Key date

Yalta and Potsdam Conferences: 1945

Key term

Yalta and Potsdam Conferences
Held respectively in February and July 1945, these were the major gatherings of the victorious Allies concerned with drawing the map of the post-war world.

Some key books on the Great Patriotic War:
Anthony Beevor, *Berlin: The Downfall 1945* (Penguin, 2002)
Anthony Beevor, *Stalingrad* (Penguin, 1998)
Chris Bellamy, *Absolute War: Soviet Russia in the Second World War* (Macmillan, 2007)
Ian Kershaw, *Fateful Choices: Ten Decisions that Changed the World* (Allen Lane, 2007)
Catherine Merridale, *Ivan's War: The Red Army 1939–45* (Faber, 2005)

Summary diagram: The Soviet Union at war, 1941–45

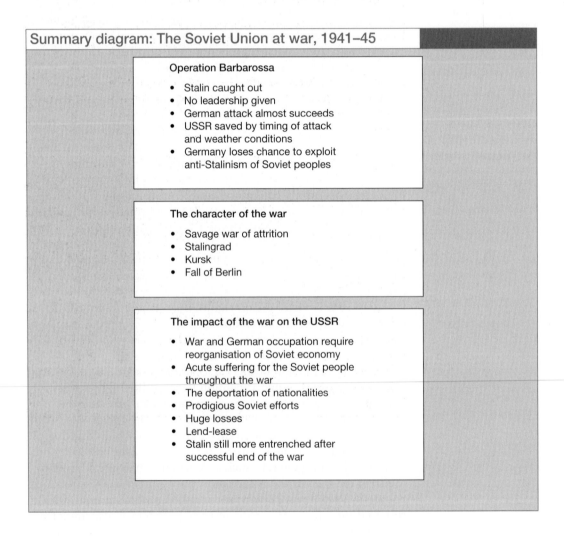

Operation Barbarossa

- Stalin caught out
- No leadership given
- German attack almost succeeds
- USSR saved by timing of attack and weather conditions
- Germany loses chance to exploit anti-Stalinism of Soviet peoples

The character of the war

- Savage war of attrition
- Stalingrad
- Kursk
- Fall of Berlin

The impact of the war on the USSR

- War and German occupation require reorganisation of Soviet economy
- Acute suffering for the Soviet people throughout the war
- The deportation of nationalities
- Prodigious Soviet efforts
- Huge losses
- Lend-lease
- Stalin still more entrenched after successful end of the war

Study Guide: AS Question

In the style of Edexcel

How far do you agree that Stalin's war leadership mainly accounts for the USSR's ability to resist the German invasion in the years 1941–43? (30 marks)

Exam tips

The cross-references are intended to take you straight to the material that will help you to answer the question.

As an early planning aid, take a sheet of A4 paper and write in a circle in the middle 'and so the USSR successfully resisted the German invasion'.

Now place the following factors around the edge of the sheet, read the relevant pages of Chapter 5, and then draw arrows to show the connections of the factors *with one another* and with the central circle.

- Hitler's misjudgements (pages 91, 92, 93)
- Nazi racism (page 92)
- 'General Winter' (page 92)
- The balance of forces (pages 91, 96)
- The pre-war organisation of the USSR's economy (page 96)
- The response of the people of the USSR (pages 96–98)
- Wartime reorganisation of the economy to meet the demands of war (pages 96, 97)
- Lend-lease (page 97)
- Military leadership (pages 91–92)
- Stalin's war leadership (pages 90–91, 93, 98, 99)

How significant does Stalin's war leadership seem to be as a result of your analysis? If you first try to see the way in which factors combined to produce an outcome, it will help you to decide which factors are crucial.

6

Life in Stalin's Russia

POINTS TO CONSIDER

The impact of Stalinism was not restricted to politics and economics. The whole of Soviet life was influenced by it. This chapter examines some of the main ways in which this occurred by exploring the following themes:

- Soviet culture
- The cult of personality
- Education
- Health
- Religion
- Women and the family
- Stalin and Stalinism.

Key dates

1926	Komsomol youth movement created
1928	New campaign of persecution of religion
1932	Stalin called for 'engineering of the human soul'
1934	Soviet Union of Writers formed
	Death of Maxim Gorky
	Imprisonment of Osip Mandelstam
1935	Soviet Academy of Sciences became the controlling body over all scholars
1936–38	Severe repression of Soviet creative artists
1936	Works of Dmitri Shostakovich banned
	New Soviet Constitution introduced
	Family laws restricting abortion, divorce and homosexuality
	'Housewives Movement' created under Stalin's patronage
1938	Imprisonment of Vsevolod Meyerhold
1939	18th Congress of the CPSU carried worship of Stalin to new heights
1940	Date by which 88 per cent of adults in the USSR were literate

1940	Date in which only 500 churches were open for worship, compared with 50,000 in 1917
1941–45	Artists enlisted in the 'Great Fatherland War' war effort
1944	New family laws introduced
1945	Soviet victory over Germany enhanced Stalin's God-like reputation
1956	Khrushchev's 'Secret Report' describes Stalin's 'cult of personality'

Key question
What was the place of culture in the USSR under Stalin?

1 | Soviet Culture

Lenin had declared that 'the purpose of art and literature is to serve the people' (see page 4). Stalin was equally determined that culture should perform a social and political role. In the Russia that he was building, the arts had to have the same driving purpose that his economic policies had. Culture was not simply a matter of refined tastes: it was an expression of society's values and had to be shaped and directed in the same way that agriculture and industry had. In creating the first truly socialist state there had to be a cultural revolution to accompany the political and economic one. It followed that the test to be applied to any aspect of culture was whether it promoted socialist values.

In practice what this came to mean was that, given the despotic power that Stalin wielded, cultural works in all their various forms, from buildings to paintings to novels to operas, had to conform to the standards set by Joseph Stalin. He became the great cultural judge and arbiter. Stalinist terror pervaded the realm of the arts, just as it did the political and industrial worlds. Artists who did not conform were as likely to be purged as politicians who were deemed to be a danger to Stalin or industrial managers who did not meet their quotas.

Key dates

Severe repression of creative artists: 1936–38

Artists enlisted in the 'Great Fatherland War' war effort: 1941–1945

Stalin called for the 'engineering of the human soul': 1932

Socialist realism

In 1932, Stalin famously declared to a gathering of Soviet writers that they were 'engineers of the human soul'. This was a highly revealing remark. What he was telling his audience was that their task was essentially a social not an artistic one. They were not to regard themselves as individuals concerned with self-expression, but as contributors to the great collective effort of reshaping the thinking and behaviour of the Soviet people.

This was a radical departure from the European tradition which had always valued the right of the artist to express himself as he wished; that was the way genuine art was created. Stalin rejected such notions. Artists were to be treated as if they were part of the industrial system; their task was to create a useful product. Self-expression had to be subordinated to the political and social needs of the new nation. It was not the individual but the people who mattered. The artist's first task was to make his work appropriate and relevant to the society he was serving. If he failed to do this he was engaging in bourgeois self-indulgence, making himself more important than the people he was meant to serve.

Writers

It is not surprising, therefore, that when the **Soviet Union of Writers** was formed in 1934 it should have declared that its first objective was to convince all writers that they must struggle for **socialist realism** in their works. This could be best achieved by conforming to a set of guidelines. Writers were to make sure that their work:

- was acceptable to the party in theme and presentation
- was written in a style and vocabulary that would be immediately understandable to the workers who would read it
- contained characters whom the readers could either identify with as socialist role models or directly recognise as examples of class enemies
- was optimistic and uplifting in its message and thus advanced the cause of socialism.

These rules applied to creative writing in all its forms: novels, plays, poems and film scripts. It was not easy for genuine writers to continue working within these restrictions, but conformity was the price of acceptance, even of survival. Before his death in 1934 Maxim Gorky (see page 8) was the leading voice among Russian writers. He used his undoubted skills to praise Stalin's First Five-Year Plan not merely as a great industrial achievement but as something of 'the highest spiritual value'. Other writers found it less easy to sell their soul. One author, **Boris Pasternak**, later celebrated in the West for his *Dr. Zhivago*, a novel that was forbidden in the USSR during his lifetime, found some way out of his dilemma by restricting himself to translating historical works into Russian.

Many others who were not prepared to compromise their artistic integrity lost their position, their liberty, and sometimes their lives. Surveillance, scrutiny and denunciations intensified throughout the 1930s. **Alexander Solzhenitsyn** spent many years in the gulag for falling foul of Stalin's censors. His documentary novels, such as *One Day in the Life of Ivan Denisovich* and *The Gulag Archipelago*, which was published after Stalin's death, described the horrific conditions in the labour camps.

In such an intimidating atmosphere suicides became common. Robert Service notes in his biography of Stalin that: 'More great intellectuals perished in the 1930s than survived.' In 1934, **Osip Mandelstam**, a leading literary figure, was informed on following a private gathering of writers at which he had recited a mocking poem about Stalin, containing the lines 'Around him, fawning half-men for him to play with, as he prates and points a finger.' Mandelstam died four years later in the gulag. He once remarked, 'Only in Russia is poetry taken seriously, so seriously men are killed for it.'

Key question
How did 'socialist realism' affect the work and lives of writers and artists?

Key terms

Soviet Union of Writers
The body having authority over all published writers. Under Stalin's direction it had the right to ban or censor any work of which it disapproved.

Socialist realism
A form of representational art which the people can understand and relate to their own lives.

Key figure

Boris Pasternak (1890–1960)
A poet, essayist and novelist – his works were regarded by the authorities as implicitly critical of the Soviet system and therefore unacceptable.

Key dates

Soviet Union of Writers formed: 1934

Death of Maxim Gorky: 1934

Imprisonment of Osip Mandelstam: 1934

Key figure

Alexander Solzhenitsyn (b. 1918)
A deeply spiritual man and writer, he was regarded by the authorities as a subversive; after his expulsion from the USSR in 1974 he became as equally critical of Western materialism as he had been of Soviet communism.

Stalin took a close personal interest in new works. One word of criticism from him was enough for a writer to be thrown out of the Union, often followed by arrest and imprisonment. Part of the tragedy was the readiness of so many second and third-rate writers to expose and bring down their betters as a means of advancing their own careers. This was a common characteristic of totalitarian regimes in the twentieth century. The atmosphere of repression and the demand for conformity elevated the mediocre to a position of influence and power. Fortunately, the coming of the war in 1941 brought some respite to the beleaguered writers since they were now able to throw themselves wholeheartedly into the task of writing heroic tales of the Russian people working for glorious victory under the beloved Stalin.

It should be noted that historians have on occasion queried whether the term 'totalitarian' should be used to describe Stalinism, their argument being that the limited technology of the time simply did not allow total control to be imposed. Yet, after allowing for that point, the fact remains that Stalin's aim in culture as in politics and economics was total conformity. And it was the aim that created the atmosphere and conditioned the way in which artists worked.

Key question
What was the impact of Stalinism on other art forms?

Other art forms

The Soviet Union of Writers set the tone for all other organisations in the arts. Painting and sculpture, film-making, opera and ballet all had to respond to the Stalinist demand for socialist realism. Abstract and experimental forms were frowned upon because they broke the rules that works should be immediately accessible and meaningful to the public. Jazz was condemned as decadent.

Key figure

Osip Mandelstam (1891–1938)
A poet and novelist, he struggled in his writings after 1917 to uphold human dignity in the face of Soviet oppression.

Theatre and film

An idea of the repression that operated can be gained from the following figures:

- In 1936–37, 68 films had to be withdrawn in mid-production and another 30 taken out of circulation.
- In the same period, 10 out of 19 plays and ballets were ordered to be withdrawn.
- In the 1937–38 theatre season, 60 plays were banned from performance, 10 theatres closed in Moscow and another 10 in Leningrad.

Key term

'Total theatre'
An approach which endeavours to break down the barriers between actors and audience by revolutionary use of lighting, sound and stage settings.

A prominent victim was the director **Vsevolod Meyerhold** (see page 106), whose concept of **'total theatre'** had a major influence on European theatre. It might be thought that Meyerhold's techniques for bringing theatre closer to the people would have perfectly fitted the notion of socialist realism. But his appeal for artistic liberty – 'The theatre is a living creative thing. We must have freedom – yes, freedom' – led to a campaign being mounted against him by the toadies who served Stalin. He was arrested in 1938. After a two-year imprisonment during which he was regularly

Key date

Imprisonment of Vsevolod Meyerhold: 1938

flogged with rubber straps until he fainted, he was shot. His name was one on a list of 346 death sentences that Stalin signed on 16 January 1940.

Even the internationally acclaimed director **Sergei Eisenstein**, whose films *Battleship Potemkin* and *October*, celebrating the revolutionary Russian proletariat, had done so much to advance the Communist cause, was heavily censured. This was because a later work of his, *Ivan the Terrible* (see page 110), was judged to be an unflattering portrait of a great Russian leader and, therefore, by implication disrespectful of Stalin.

Painting and sculpture

Painters and sculptors were left in no doubt as to what was required of them. Their duty to conform to socialist realism in their style and at the same time honour their mighty leader was captured in an article in the art magazine *Iskusstvo* commenting on a painting that had won a Stalin prize in 1948.

> On a bright morning Comrade Stalin is seen walking in the vast collective farm fields with high-voltage power transmission lines in the distance. His exalted face and his whole figure are lit with the golden rays of springtime sun. The image of Comrade Stalin is the triumphant march of communism, the symbol of courage, the symbol of the Soviet people's glory, calling for new heroic exploits for the benefit of our great motherland.

Music

Since music is an essentially abstract form of art, it was more difficult for the Soviet censors to make composers respond to Stalin's notions of social realism. Nevertheless, it was the art form which most interested Stalin, who regarded himself as something of an expert in the field. He claimed to be able to recognise socialist music when he heard it and to know what type of song would inspire the people. He had many a battle with the Soviet Union's leading composer, **Dmitri Shostakovich**, who had a chequered career under Stalinism. In 1936, Shostakovich's opera, *Lady Macbeth of Mzensk*, was banned on the grounds that it was 'bourgeois and formalistic'. In the same year, his fourth symphony was withdrawn from the repertoire for similar reasons.

However, as with a number of writers, the war gave Shostakovich the opportunity to express his deep patriotism. His powerful seventh symphony, composed during the siege of Leningrad in 1941, was a highly dramatic and stirring piece, depicting in sound the courageous struggle and final victory of the people of the city. At the end of the war, in return for being reinstated, he promised to bring his music closer to 'the folk art of the people'. This left him artistically freer than he had been before, though Stalin was still apt to criticise some of his new works. Shostakovich's growing international reputation helped protect him.

Key figures

Vsevolod Meyerhold (1874–1940)
Despite the international reputation he achieved, his innovatory theatrical methods meant he was never trusted by Lenin or Stalin.

Sergei Eisenstein (1898–1948)
An outstanding figure in world cinema; his use of light and shade in the creation of atmosphere and spectacle left a permanent mark on film as a popular art form.

Dmitri Shostakovich (1906–75)
The composer spent his creative life trying to keep one step ahead of the censors by exploiting their musical ignorance; he managed to survive Stalin and became recognised as one of the twentieth century's great composers.

Key date

Works of Dmitri Shostakovich banned: 1936

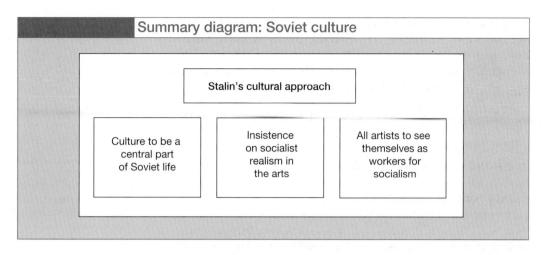

Summary diagram: Soviet culture

Stalin's cultural approach

Culture to be a central part of Soviet life

Insistence on socialist realism in the arts

All artists to see themselves as workers for socialism

2 | The Cult of Personality

Key question
How did Stalin build up a cult of personality?

Adolf Hitler once wrote that 'the personality cult is the best form of government'. It is not certain whether Stalin ever read this but it would be a fitting commentary on his leadership of the Soviet Union. One of the strongest charges made by Nikita Khrushchev in his attack on Stalin's record was that he had indulged in the cult of personality (see page 129). He was referring to the way Stalin dominated every aspect of Soviet life, so that he became not simply a leader but the embodiment of the nation itself. Similarly, the Communist Party became indistinguishable from Stalin himself as a person. Communism was no longer a set of theories; it was no longer Leninism. It was whatever Stalin said and did. Soviet Communism was Stalinism.

From the 1930s on, Stalin's picture began to appear everywhere. Every newspaper, book and film, no matter what its theme, carried a reference to Stalin's greatness. Every achievement of the USSR was credited to Stalin. Such was his all-pervasive presence that Soviet Communism became personalised around him. On occasion, in private, Stalin protested that he did not seek the glorification he received but, significantly, he made no effort to prevent it.

Ironically, in view of his later denunciation of Stalin, it was Khrushchev who did as much as anyone to promote the image of Stalin as a glorious hero. At the trial of Zinoviev and Kamenev in August 1936, he cursed the defendants as 'Miserable pigmies!' and went on:

> They lifted their hands against the greatest of all men, our wise *vozhd*, Comrade Stalin. Thou, Comrade Stalin, has raised the great banner of Marxism–Leninism high over the entire world and carried it forward. We assure thee, Comrade Stalin, that the Moscow Bolshevik organisation will increase Stalinist vigilance still more, will extirpate the Trotskyite–Zinovievite clique and close the ranks of the party around the great Stalin.

Key date
New Soviet Constitution introduced: 1936

Khrushchev was the first to coin the term 'Stalinism' in 1936 at the introduction of the new Soviet Constitution: 'Our constitution is the Marxism–Leninism–Stalinism that has conquered one sixth of the globe.' At the trial of Pyatakov and others, before an audience calculated by *Pravda* as being 200,000 in number, Khrushchev declared:

> By lifting their hands against Comrade Stalin they lifted them against all the best that humanity possesses. For Stalin is hope, Stalin is expectation; he is the beacon that guides all progressive mankind. Stalin is our banner! Stalin is our will! Stalin is our victory!

At the 18th Congress of the CPSU in March 1939, Khrushchev lauded the Soviet leader as 'our great inspiration, our beloved Stalin', extolling him as 'the greatest genius of humanity, teacher and *vozhd* who leads us towards Communism'.

Key date

18th Congress of the CPSU carried worship of Stalin to new heights: 1939

'Under the leadership of the Great Stalin, Forward to Communism!'

'Thank you, dear Stalin, for our happy childhood!'

Posters from the 1930s, typical of the propaganda of the time, showing Stalin as the leader of his adoring people. Poster art was a very effective way for the Stalinist authorities to put their message across. In what ways do the posters illustrate the artistic notion of socialist realism?

It is one of the many paradoxes of Soviet history that the Communist movement, which in theory drew its authority from the will of the masses, became so dependent on the idea of the great leader. Such was Stalin's standing and authority that he transcended politics. Since he represented not simply the Party but the nation itself, he became the personification of all that was best in Russia. This was an extraordinary achievement for a Georgian and it produced a further remarkable development. It became common to assert that many of the great achievements in world history were the work of Russians. The claims reached ridiculous proportions: that Shakespeare was really a Russian, that Russian navigators had been the first Europeans to discover America and that Russian mathematicians had discovered the secrets of the atom long before Einstein. Eventually Stalin overreached himself. Given a bottle of Coca-Cola at the Potsdam Conference by President Truman, Stalin ordered his scientists to come up with a Russian drink to match it. They tried but finally had to admit that, while Soviet science could achieve the impossible, miracles were beyond it.

Propaganda

Key question
How was state propaganda used to promote Stalin's image?

The cult of personality was not a spontaneous response of the people. It did not come from below; it was imposed from above. The image of Stalin as hero and saviour of the Soviet people was manufactured. It was a product of the Communist Party machine which controlled all the main forms of information – newspapers, cinema and radio. Roy Medvedev, a Soviet historian, who lived through Stalinism, later explained:

> Stalin did not rely on terror alone, but also on the support of the majority of the people; effectively deceived by cunning propaganda, they gave Stalin credit for the successes of others and even for 'achievements' that were in fact totally fictitious.

A fascinating example of building on the fictitious was the Stakhanovite movement (see page 50). It is now generally accepted that the official claim made in August 1935 that the miner, Alexei Stakhanov, had individually hewn 14 times his required quota of coal in one shift was a fabrication. Nevertheless, so well was the story presented and developed by the authorities at the time that his achievement became a contemporary legend, illustrating what heights of endeavour could be reached by selfless workers responding to the appeals and the example of their great leader.

Worship of Stalin

Key term

Icons
Two-dimensional representations of Jesus Christ and the saints: the power and beauty of its icons is one of the great glories of the Orthodox Church.

Despite the Soviet attack on the Church, the powerful religious sense of the Russian people remained and it was cleverly exploited by the authorities. Traditional worship with its veneration of the saints, its **icons**, prayers and incantations, translated easily into the new regime. Stalin became an icon. This was literally true. His picture was carried on giant flags in processions. A French visitor watching at one of the **May Day** celebrations in Moscow's Red Square was staggered by the sight of a fly-past of planes all trailing huge portraits of Stalin. 'My God!' he exclaimed. 'Exactly, Monsieur,' said his Russian guide.

However, even May Day came to take second place to the celebration of Stalin's birthday each December. Beginning in 1929 on his fiftieth birthday, the occasion was turned each year into the greatest celebration in the Soviet calendar. Day-long parades in Red Square of marching troops, rolling tanks, dancing children and applauding workers, all presided over by an occasionally smiling Stalin high on a rostrum overlooking Lenin's tomb, became the high moment of the year. It was a new form of tsar worship.

Stalin's wisdom and brilliance were extolled daily in Pravda and *Isvestiya*, the official Soviet newspapers. Hardly an article appeared in any journal that did not include the obligatory reference to his greatness. Children learned from their earliest moments to venerate Stalin as the provider of all good things. At school they were taught continually and in all subjects that Stalin was their guide and protector. It was an interesting aspect of the prescribed school curriculum (see page 114) that history was to be taught not as 'an abstract sociological scheme' but as a chronological story full of stirring tales of the great Russian heroes of the past, such as **Ivan the Terrible** and **Peter the Great**, leading up to the triumph of Lenin and the Bolsheviks in 1917. The climax of this story was Stalin, who, building on the work of Lenin, was securing and extending the Soviet Union. This adulation of Stalin was not confined to history books. There were no text books in any subject that did not praise the virtues of Stalin, the master builder of the Soviet nation, inspiration to his people and glorious model for struggling peoples everywhere.

Eulogies of Stalin poured off the press, each one trying to outbid the other in its veneration of the leader. Typical of the tone and contents was an official biography published by a group of Soviet writers in 1947:

> Stalin guides the destinies of a multi-national Socialist state. His advice is taken as a guide to action in all fields of Socialist construction. His work is extraordinary for its variety; his energy truly amazing. The range of questions which engage his attention is immense. Stalin is wise and deliberate in solving complex political questions where a thorough weighing of pros and cons is required. At the same time, he is a supreme master of bold revolutionary decisions and of swift adaptations to changed conditions. Stalin is the Lenin of today.

Komsomol

A particularly useful instrument for the spread of Stalinist propaganda was **Komsomol**, a youth movement which had begun in Lenin's time but was created as a formal body in 1926 under the direct control of the CPSU. Among its main features were:

Key terms

May Day ('Labour Day')
1 May, traditionally regarded as a special day for honouring the workers and the achievements of socialism.

Isvestiya
Translates as 'The Times'.

Komsomol
The Communist Union of Youth.

Key figures

Ivan the Terrible (reigned 1547–84)
A powerful tsar who considerably extended Russian territory through conquest.

Peter the Great (reigned 1689–1725)
A reforming tsar who attempted to modernise his nation by incorporating Western European ways.

Key date

Komsomol youth movement created: 1926

- It was open to those aged between 14 and 28 (a Young Pioneer movement existed for those under 14).
- It pledged itself totally to Stalin and the Party (in this regard it paralleled the Hitler Youth in Nazi Germany).
- Membership was not compulsory but its attraction to young people was that it offered them the chance of eventual full membership of the CPSU with all the privileges that went with it.
- It grew from two million members in 1927 to 10 million in 1940.

The idealism of the young was very effectively exploited by Stalin's regime. Komsomol members were among the most enthusiastic supporters of the Five-Year Plans, as they proved by going off in their thousands to help build the new industrial cities such as Magnitogorsk (see page 46). It was Komsomol who provided the flag-wavers and the cheerleaders and who organised the huge gymnastic displays that were the centrepieces of the massive parades on May Day and Stalin's birthday.

Every political gathering was a study in the advancement of the Stalin cult. The exaggeration and the sycophantic character of it all is clear in the following extract from a speech given by a delegate to the Seventh Congress of Soviets in 1935.

> Thank you, Stalin. Thank you because I am joyful. Thank you because I am well. Centuries will pass, and the generations still to come will regard us as the happiest of mortals, because we lived in the century of centuries, because we were privileged to see Stalin, our inspired leader. Yes and we regard ourselves as the happiest of mortals because we are the contemporaries of a man who never had an equal in world history.
>
> The men of all ages will call on thy name, which is strong, beautiful, wise and marvellous. Thy name is engraven on every factory, every machine, every place on the earth and in the hearts of all men.

Stalin's popularity

Key question
How popular was Stalin in the Soviet Union?

It is difficult to judge how popular Stalin was in real terms. The applause that greeted his every appearance in public or in cinema newsreels was more likely to have been a matter of prudence than of real affection. The same is true of the tears shed by thousands at his passing in 1953. There was no way in which criticism or opposition could be voiced. The gulag was full of comrades who had spoken out of turn.

The intense **political correctness** of the day required that Stalin be publicly referred to as the faultless leader and inspirer of the nation. He made occasional broadcasts, but he was no orator. He could never match Hitler's gift for arousing an audience or Churchill's for inspiring one. In wartime it was the gravity of the situation that gave Stalin's broadcasts their power. Perhaps it was Stalin's own recognition of his limitations in this regard that explains why after 1945 he made only three public speeches and these were only a few minutes long. Yet in an odd way Stalin's remoteness helped promote his image. Seen as a distant figure on

Key term

Political correctness
The requirement that people conform to a prescribed set of opinions when expressing themselves, to show that they have accepted the ideology of the leaders of society.

a high rostrum or in the selected views of him in the official newsreels, he retained a powerful mystique.

A fascinating insight into Stalin's standing with his own people was provided by **Leon Feuchtwanger**, the German writer and a visitor to the Soviet Union in the 1930s, who was over-impressed by Stalin's apparent economic successes but who remained a shrewd observer of Soviet attitudes. Writing in 1937, he explained the particular character of Stalin's popularity in these terms:

Leon Feuchtwanger (1884–1958) Jewish novelist and literary critic who was exiled from Nazi Germany in the 1930s.

Key figure

> The people were grateful to Stalin for their bread and meat, for the order in their lives, for their education and for creating their army which secured this new well-being. The people have to have someone to whom to express their gratitude, and for this purpose they do not select an abstract concept, such as 'communism', but a real man, Stalin. Their unbounded reverence is consequently not for Stalin, but for him as a symbol of the patently successful economic reconstruction.

Researchers from a later generation, such as Sheila Fitzpatrick, aware of how little Stalin had done to improve the conditions of the Soviet people, offer a different slant:

> Judging by the NKVD's soundings of public opinion, the Stalinist regime was relatively, though not desperately, unpopular in Russian towns. (In Russian villages, especially in the first half of the 1930s, its unpopularity was much greater.) Overall, as the NKVD regularly reported, the ordinary 'little man' in Soviet towns, who thought only of his own and his family's welfare, was 'dissatisfied with Soviet Power', though in a somewhat fatalistic and passive manner. The post NEP situation was compared unfavourably with NEP, and Stalin – despite the officially fostered Stalin cult – was compared unfavourably with Lenin, sometimes because he was more repressive but often because he let people go hungry.

The USSR's triumph in the 'Great Fatherland War' of 1941–45 did much to perpetuate the image of Stalin as national hero. Whatever doubts might have been whispered about Stalin before the war became scarcely possible to consider let alone utter after 1945. The Soviet Union's triumph over Germany in 1945 was a supreme moment in Russian history. Under Stalin, the nation had survived perhaps the most savage conflict in European history. This gave him a prestige as the nation's saviour that mattered far more than whether he was simply liked. The important point was that the Soviet people held him in even greater awe and fear than before. And, as the tsars had always known, it does not matter whether a regime is loved as long as it is feared.

Soviet victory over Germany enhanced Stalin's God-like reputation: 1945

Key date

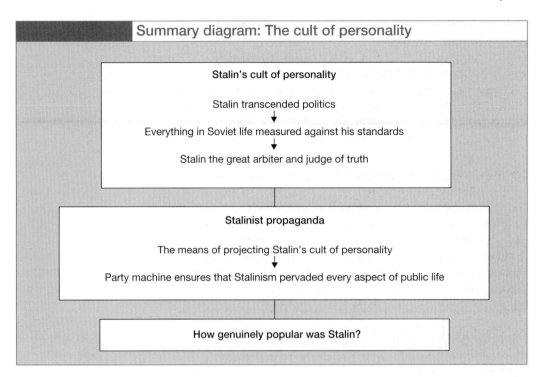

Summary diagram: The cult of personality

Stalin's cult of personality

Stalin transcended politics
↓
Everything in Soviet life measured against his standards
↓
Stalin the great arbiter and judge of truth

Stalinist propaganda

The means of projecting Stalin's cult of personality
↓
Party machine ensures that Stalinism pervaded every aspect of public life

How genuinely popular was Stalin?

Key question
Why was Stalin so
determined to reform
the Soviet education
system?

3 | Education

The initial attitudes of Lenin and the Bolsheviks when they came
to power were shaped by their general desire to reject bourgeois
standards. In the field of education this led to an attack on book
learning and traditional academic subjects. For a brief period text
books were thrown away, exams abolished, and schools either shut
altogether or opened only for a limited number of days. Young
people were encouraged to learn trades and engage in activities
that were of practical value.

But by the time Stalin came to power it was generally accepted
that the dismissal of the old ways had gone too far. As in so many
areas of Russian life, Stalin reversed the trends initiated by the
Bolsheviks after 1917. His driving aim was to modernise the
Soviet Union and he believed that to achieve this the population,
especially the young, must be made literate. He was aware of the
complaints of parents and employers that young people were
entering the workplace without having mastered the basic skills
in reading and writing. To meet this crippling problem, formal
education was made a priority. The need for discipline and order
was stressed. It made little sense to insist on strict rules of
conduct for workers in the factories, if schools allowed pupils to
behave in a free and easy manner. The education system must
develop the same serious, committed attitude that prevailed in
the workplace.

Key features of the education system developed under Stalin

- Ten years of compulsory schooling for all children.
- Core curriculum laid down: reading, writing, mathematics, science, history, geography, Russian (and for the national minorities their native language), Marxist theory.
- State-prescribed text books to be used.
- Homework to be a regular requirement.
- State-organised tests and examinations.
- School uniforms made compulsory (girls were obliged to have their hair in pigtails).
- Fees to be charged for the last three years (ages 15–18) of non-compulsory secondary schooling.

The emphasis on regulation was not accidental. The intention behind these requirements, which were introduced during the 1930s, was to create a disciplined, trained generation of young people fully ready to join the workforce which was engaged through the Five-Year Plans in constructing the new Communist society.

Results of the reforms

The results of these education policies were impressive:

- Between 1929 and 1940 the number of children attending school rose from 12 million to 35 million.
- By 1939, schooling for 8- to 14-year-olds had become universal in the urban areas.
- Between 1926 and 1940 the literacy rate for the population over the age of nine increased from 51 per cent to 88 per cent.

Date by which 88 per cent of adults in the USSR were literate: 1940

Key date

An egalitarian system?

The introduction of fees for the last three years of schooling (see above) may appear to challenge the notion of an egalitarian education system. But the official justification for it was that all societies, including socialist ones, need a trained section of the community to serve the people in expert ways. Doctors, managers, scientists, administrators and the like clearly required particular training in order to be able to fill that social role. Those who stayed on at school after 15 were obviously young people of marked ability who would eventually go on to university to become the specialists of the future. This was undeniably a selection process, but the argument was that it was selection by ability, not, as in the corrupt tsarist days or in the decadent capitalist world, by class. Moreover, the requirement to pay fees would not prove an obstacle since there were many grants and scholarships in the gift of the government, the Party and the trade unions.

Key question
Was the education system genuinely egalitarian?

The role of the elite

That was the official line. But behind the undoubted rise in educational standards and the marked increase in literacy rates, the system was creating a privileged elite. This was one of the paradoxes of revolutionary Russia. Before 1917 the Bolsheviks had poured scorn on the bourgeois governing elites that monopolised power in all capitalist societies. But the equivalent very quickly developed in Soviet Russia. The intelligentsia that formed the nomenklatura appreciated that education was the key to opportunity; that is why they took great pains to ensure that their children received the best form of it. Private tuition and private education became normal for the elite of Soviet society.

The unfair and un-socialist nature of all this was covered up by claims that the schools were 'specialist' institutions for children with particular aptitudes, rather than a matter of privilege. The Party had the right to nominate those who were to receive the higher grade training that would give them access to university. As university education expanded, it was Party members or their children who had the first claim on the best places. In the period 1928–32, for example, a third of all undergraduates were Party nominees. As graduates, they were then invited to enter one or other of the three key areas of Soviet administration – industry, the civil service or the armed services. This educational and promotional process had an important political aspect. It enhanced Stalin's power by creating a class of privileged administrators who had every motive for supporting him since they were his creatures. Osip Mandelstam, the disgraced poet (see page 105), described this precisely:

> At the end of the twenties and in the thirties our authorities, making no concession to 'egalitarianism', started to raise the living standards of those who had proved their usefulness. Everybody was concerned to keep the material benefits he had worked so hard to earn. A thin layer of privileged people gradually came into being with **'packets'**, country villas and cars. Those who had been granted a share of the cake eagerly did everything asked of them.

Key term

'Packets'
Privileges and special benefits.

Key question
How did Soviet scholars respond to the demands of Stalinism?

Key date

Soviet Academy of Sciences came under state control. 1935

Universities

In intellectual terms, the Soviet Union's most prestigious institution was the Academy of Sciences. Based on the famed tsarist Imperial Academy, it became in the new Russia an umbrella body incorporating all the major research organisations, some 250 in number with over 50,000 individual members. The term 'sciences' translates broadly to cover all the main intellectual and scientific streams: the arts, agriculture, medicine, management. All the major scholars in their fields were academicians. In 1935 the Academy was brought under direct government control. In return for increased academic and social privileges, it pledged itself totally to Stalin in his building of the new Communist society. What this meant in practice was that all the academicians would henceforth produce work wholly in keeping with Stalinist values. They would become politically correct.

One distressing aspect of this was that Soviet historians no longer engaged in genuine historical research and analysis. Their reputation and acceptance as scholars depended on their presenting history shaped and interpreted as Stalin wanted.

They ceased to be historians in any meaningful sense and became intellectual lackeys of the regime.

The Lysenko affair

Where such academic subservience could lead was evident in an infamous case which damaged Soviet science and agriculture for decades. In the 1930s, **Trofim Lysenko**, a quack geneticist, claimed to have discovered ways of developing 'super-crops', which would grow in any season and produce a yield anything up to 16 times greater than the harvests produced by traditional methods. Stalin, who had convinced himself that there was such a thing as 'socialist science', which was superior to that practised in the bourgeois West, was excited by Lysenko's claims and gave him his full support. This meant that, although the claims were in fact wholly false, based on rigged experiments and doctored figures, Lysenko was unchallengeable by his colleagues. Those who dared protest that his methods were faulty were removed from their posts and dumped in the gulag.

It was not until 1965, many years after Stalin's death in 1953, that Lysenko's ideas were finally exposed in the Soviet Union for the nonsense they were. The tragedy was that by then they had played a part in creating the famines that so frequently ravaged Stalin's Soviet Union.

Key question
What was the importance of the Lysenko affair?

Key figure

Trofim Lysenko (1898–1976)
Appointed head of the Soviet Academy of Agricultural Sciences, he hounded those biologists who dared point out the absurdity of his theories.

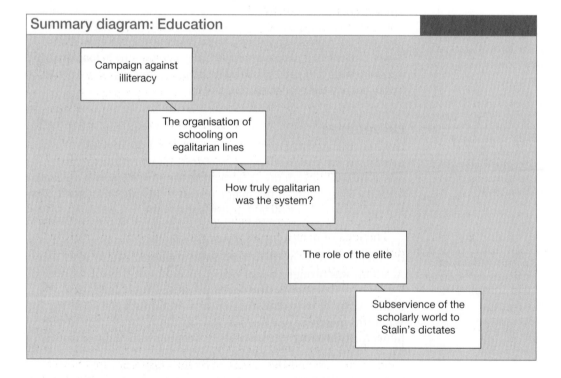

Summary diagram: Education

Campaign against illiteracy

The organisation of schooling on egalitarian lines

How truly egalitarian was the system?

The role of the elite

Subservience of the scholarly world to Stalin's dictates

Key question
How effectively did the Soviet Union develop a public health service?

Key terms

Infant mortality
A calculation of the number of children who die per 100 or per 1000 of all those in a particular age group.

Tuberculosis
A wasting disease, often affecting the lungs, which was especially prevalent in Russia.

4 | Health

In 1918 Lenin's Bolshevik government had set up the People's Commissariat of Health. Its aim was nothing less than to provide a free health service for all the people. The Commissariat continued to operate in Stalin's time with the same objective. But, from the beginning, the sad fact was that Soviet Russia never had the resources to match its intentions. The disruptions of the civil war period made it impossible to develop a structured health service on the lines originally envisaged. Things picked up in the better economic conditions produced by the NEP. **Infant mortality** dropped and the spread of contagious diseases was checked. But famine remained a constant threat.

In the 1930s, the collectivisation policy enforced by Stalin created the largest famine in Russian history. This made the worst hit areas – Ukraine and Kazakhstan – places of death and disease. Such was the scale of the horror that the existing health services in those regions simply could not cope. Although some parts of the USSR were relatively unscathed, it proved impossible to transfer medical supplies from these areas on a big enough scale to provide real help to the stricken regions. There was also the chilling fact that since Stalin refused to acknowledge that there was a famine, no real effort was made by the central government to deal with its consequences.

Areas of improvement

It is true that in the unaffected areas in the 1930s there was a genuine advance in health standards. The number of qualified doctors and nurses increased and, while the benefits of this may not have reached the majority of the population, there were spectacular successes which were made much of in Stalinist propaganda. Sanatoria, for the treatment of **tuberculosis**, and rest and retirement homes for the workers, were created. There were even holiday centres in such places as Yalta on the Black Sea where selected workers were sent as a reward for their efforts. However, the number who enjoyed such treatment was a tiny fraction of the workforce. The main beneficiaries of improved medical care were not ordinary Russians but Party members and the nomenklatura. It was one of the privileges of belonging to the political establishment.

The idea of health for all was never abandoned, but it proved difficult to maintain it as a priority during the headlong push for industrial growth in the 1930s. It is true that factories and plants were urged to provide crèches so that more mothers with young children could be employed, but this was done primarily to meet the needs of industry not those of the mother. Childcare at the factories was regimented by such measures as the requirement that breast feeding took place at a given time so as not to interfere with production. One positive result of Stalin's insistence that Soviet women see their primary role as mothers producing babies for the nation was the setting up of clinics and a general improvement in the standards of midwifery and gynaecology.

The impact of living conditions on health

A major barrier to improved public health was the lack of living space for most Soviet families. Nearly all workers lived in overcrowded apartments. Public housing policy had led to the building of a large number of tenement blocks in towns and cities. These were usually five-storey structures with no lifts. Quite apart from their grey, depressing appearance, they were a hazard to health. So great was the overcrowding that it was common for young families to live with their in-laws, and equally common for four or five families to share a single lavatory and a single kitchen, which was often no more than an alcove with a gas-ring. There were rotas for the use of these facilities. Queuing to use the lavatory or to cook was part of the daily routine.

Such teeming conditions did not necessarily mean a dramatic number of deaths but it did seriously lower the quality of life and made the spread of milder infections such as the common cold and influenza, and contagions like ring-worm and head-lice, extremely difficult to control.

Health in wartime

The war of 1941–45 intensified Soviet health problems. The already meagre diet was further restricted by the rationing that had to be imposed. The experience for the people in German-occupied areas or in the regions under siege was unremittingly grim. The German seizure of the USSR's most productive regions denied vital food supplies to the Soviet people. Over six million civilian deaths were the result of starvation (see page 98). In such circumstances it became meaningless to talk of public health.

There was no great improvement after the war. Stalin's concerns were industrial recovery and national defence. The annual budgets down to his death in 1953 showed a decline in the amount dedicated to improving health standards. Rationing was formally ended in 1947 but this did not mean that shortages had been genuinely overcome. Without the existence of a widespread black market, which was officially condemned by the authorities but in practice tolerated and, indeed, encouraged by them, the workers would not have been able to supplement their meagre food and fuel supplies. Accommodation was scarcer and conditions in the factories were grimmer than they had been in wartime. Real wages were not permitted to rise above **subsistence level** and the rigours of the '**Labour Code**' were not relaxed. When Stalin died in 1953 the lot of the Russian worker was harsher than at any time since 1917.

How healthy the Soviet people were under Stalin is not easy to measure precisely. The famines of the 1920s and 1930s were so frequent and severe and the horrors of the war period so grim that the question is largely irrelevant. The USSR under Stalin never formally abandoned its dream of creating a health service to outmatch that of the capitalist West. There were certainly organised attempts to train doctors, build hospitals, and improve the health and hygiene of the workers. It should also be added that in some particular areas of medical research, eye surgery for

Key question
How did living conditions affect the health of the Soviet workers?

Key question
What impact did the war have on health standards?

Key terms

Subsistence level
The bare minimum required to sustain life.

Labour Code
Severe restrictions on the right of workers to ask for better wages or conditions or to challenge the work practices and production quotas assigned to them.

example, the USSR led the world. But circumstances never allowed Stalin to pay more than lip-service to the notion of a fully funded, comprehensive system of medical provision for the people. The simple fact was that as long as the Soviet Union could not feed its people adequately – and this was the case throughout the whole period of Stalinism – the idea of an effective health service remained an aspiration but was never a reality.

This survey should not close without reference to the millions of innocent Soviet citizens starved and worked to death in Stalin's gulag. To them, talk of a health policy under Stalin would have been a black and bitter joke.

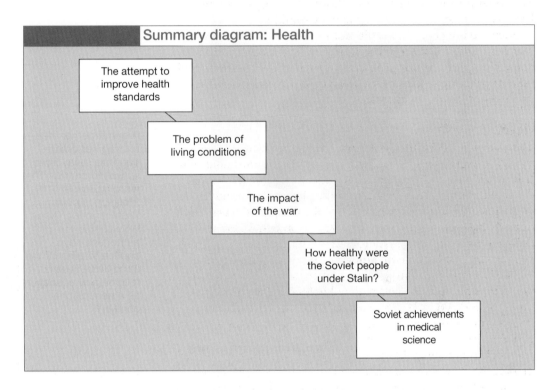

Summary diagram: Health

The attempt to improve health standards

The problem of living conditions

The impact of the war

How healthy were the Soviet people under Stalin?

Soviet achievements in medical science

Key question
What was the role of religion and the Orthodox Church in Stalin's Russia?

Key date

New campaign of religious persecution: 1928

5 | Religion

An organised attack on religion had been launched in Lenin's time (see page 6). This was renewed under Stalin who, despite his own training as a priest and his mother's profound religious devotion, shared his predecessor's view that religion had no place in a socialist society.

Coinciding with the beginning of the First Five-Year Plan in 1928, a new campaign against the churches began. The Orthodox Church was again the main target but all religions and denominations were at risk. Along with the prohibition on Orthodox churches and monasteries went the closure of synagogues and mosques. Clerics who refused to co-operate were arrested; thousands in Moscow and Leningrad were sent into exile.

The timing was not accidental. Stalin's drive for industrialisation was on such an epic scale that it required the commitment of the whole nation. That was why the purges became an accompaniment of it (see page 69). Conformity was essential and had to be imposed. Religion, with its other-worldly values, was seen as an affront to the collective needs of the nation.

A grandmother tries to drag her grand-daughter away from school to church. The wording reads: 'Religion is poison. Protect your children.' Why should the authorities have chosen to present the struggle between religion and education as a generational conflict?

The suppression of religion in the urban areas proved a fairly straightforward affair. It was a different story in the countryside. The destruction of the rural churches and the confiscation of the relics and icons that most peasants had in their homes led to revolts in many areas. What particularly angered local people was the carrying away of the church bells. The authorities had failed to understand that what to their secular mind were merely superstitious practices were to the peasants a precious part of the traditions which shaped their daily lives.

The result was widespread resistance across the rural provinces of the USSR. The authorities responded by declaring that those who opposed the restrictions on religion were really doing so in order to resist collectivisation. This allowed the requisition squads to brand the religious protesters as 'Kulaks' and to seize their property. Priests were publicly humiliated by being forced to perform demeaning tasks in public, such as clearing out pigsties and latrines.

Such was the misery the suppression created that Stalin instructed his officials to ease off. This was not through compassion. The severity of the anti-religious programme had

Key terms

Laity
The ordinary people who attend church services.

Seminaries
Training colleges for priests.

Key question
How did the war of 1941–45 alter Stalin's attitude towards the Church?

Key date
Date in which only 500 churches were open for worship, compared with 50,000 in 1917: 1940

attracted worldwide attention. In March 1930, in protest against the persecutions, Pope Pius XI announced a special day of prayer throughout the Catholic Church. For diplomatic reasons, Stalin judged it prudent to take a softer line. But this was only temporary. In the late 1930s, as part of the Great Terror, the assault on religion was renewed. Some 800 higher clergy and 4000 ordinary priests were imprisoned, along with many thousands of the **laity**. By 1940 only 500 churches were open for worship in the Soviet Union – one per cent of the figure for 1917.

The impact of the Great Patriotic War

The war which began for the USSR in June 1941 brought a respite in the persecution of the churches. Stalin was aware of how deep the religious instinct was in the great majority of Russians. While official policy was to denigrate and ridicule religion at every opportunity, and the leading Communists were always anxious to display their distaste for it, there were occasions when it proved highly useful to the authorities. Wartime provided such an occasion. Stalin was shrewd enough to enlist religion in fighting the Great Patriotic War. The churches were reopened, the clergy released and the people encouraged to celebrate the great church ceremonies.

The majestic grandeur of the Orthodox liturgy provided a huge emotional and spiritual uplift. There are few things more nerve-tinglingly exciting than a Russian church congregation in full voice. Those besieged in Leningrad recorded that while worship did not lessen their hunger or soften the German bombardment, it lifted their morale and strengthened their resolve to endure the unendurable.

What is particularly fascinating and revealing is that for the period of the war the Soviet authorities under Stalin played down politics and emphasised nationalism. Talk of the proletarian struggle gave way to an appeal to defend holy Russia against the godless invaders.

Church leaders responded as Stalin had intended. Bishops and priests turned their services into patriotic gatherings. Sermons and prayers expressed passionate defiance towards the Germans and the people were urged to rally behind their great leader, Stalin, in a supreme war effort. The reward for the Church's co-operation was a lifting of the anti-religious persecution. The improved Church–state relations continued after the war. By the time of Stalin's death in 1953, 25,000 churches had reopened along with a number of monasteries and **seminaries**.

However, this did not represent any real freedom for the Orthodox Church. The price for being allowed to exist openly was its total subservience to the regime. In 1946 Stalin required that all the Christian denominations in the Soviet Union come under the authority of the Orthodox Church, which was made responsible for ensuring that organised religion did not become a source of political opposition. It was an inglorious period for the Church. Lacking the will to resist, it became, in effect, an arm of government. Its leaders, obsequiously carrying out Stalin's orders, were barely distinguishable from the nomenklatura.

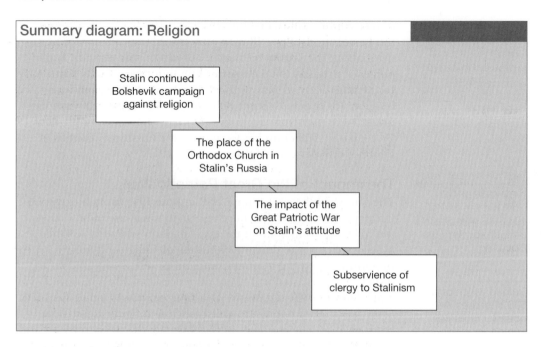

Summary diagram: Religion

Stalin continued Bolshevik campaign against religion

The place of the Orthodox Church in Stalin's Russia

The impact of the Great Patriotic War on Stalin's attitude

Subservience of clergy to Stalinism

6 | Women and the Family

Key question
Why did Stalin reverse the earlier Bolshevik policies regarding women and the family?

In keeping with their Marxist rejection of marriage as a bourgeois institution, Lenin's Bolsheviks had made divorce easier and had attempted to liberate women from the bondage of children and family. However, after only a brief experiment along these lines, Lenin's government had come to doubt its earlier enthusiasm for sweeping change in this area (see page 7). Stalin shared these doubts. Indeed, by the time he was fully installed in power in the 1930s, he was convinced that the earlier Bolshevik social experiment had failed.

By the end of the 1930s the Soviet divorce rate was the highest in Europe, running at one divorce for every two marriages. This led Stalin to embark on what Sheila Fitzpatrick has called 'the great retreat'. He began to stress the value of the family as a stabilising influence in society. He let it be known that he did not approve of the sexual freedoms that had followed the 1917 Revolution, claiming, with some justification, that Lenin himself had disapproved of the free love movement that had developed around such figures as Alexandra Kollontai (see page 8). Stalin argued that a good Communist was a socially responsible one, who took the duties of parenthood and family life seriously: 'a poor husband and father, a poor wife and mother, cannot be good citizens'.

It was as if Stalin, aware of the social upheavals his modernisation programme was causing, was trying to create some form of balance by emphasising the traditional social values attaching to the role of women as home-makers and child-raisers. He was also greatly exercised by the number of orphaned children living on the streets of the urban areas. They were the victims of the disruption caused by the civil war, collectivisation, and the growth in illegitimacy that resulted from the greater amount of casual sex. The orphanages set up to care for them had been overwhelmed by sheer numbers. Left to fend for themselves, the children had formed themselves into gangs of scavengers attacking and robbing passers-by. Disorder of this kind further convinced Stalin of the need to re-establish family values.

Main policies

Stalin's first major move came in June 1936 with a decree that reversed much of earlier Bolshevik social policy:

- unregistered marriages were no longer recognised
- divorce was made more difficult
- right to abortion severely restricted
- the family declared to be the basis of Soviet society
- homosexuality outlawed.

Conscious of both the falling birthrate and of how many Russians were dying in the Great Patriotic War, the authorities introduced measures in July 1944 re-affirming the importance of the family in Communist Russia and giving incentives to women to have large numbers of children:

- restrictions on divorce tightened still further
- abortion totally outlawed
- mothers with more than two children were to be made 'heroines of the Soviet Union'
- taxes increased on parents with fewer than two children
- the right to inherit family property was re-established.

Status of Soviet women

One group that certainly felt they had lost out were the female members of the Party and the intelligentsia, who, like Kollontai, had welcomed the Revolution as the beginning of female liberation. However, the strictures on sexual freedom under Stalin, and the emphasis on family and motherhood, allowed little room for the notion of the independent, self-sufficient female. Such gains as the feminists had made were undermined by Stalin's appeal for the nation to act selflessly in its hour of need.

It is true that Soviet propaganda spoke of the true equality of women but there was a patronising air about much that went on. **Zhenotdel**, set up under Lenin as an organisation to represent the views of the Party's female members, was allowed to lapse in 1930 on the grounds that its work was done. A 'Housewives' Movement' was created in 1936 under Stalin's patronage. Composed largely of the wives of high-ranking industrialists and managers, it set itself the task of 'civilising' the tastes and improving the conditions of the workers.

In a less fevered age this might have made some impact, but, as with all the movements of Stalin's time, it has to be set against the desperate struggle in which the USSR was engaged. Stalin continually spoke of the nation being under siege and of the need to build a war economy. This made any movement not directly concerned with industrial production or defence seem largely irrelevant. Most of the women's organisations fell into this category.

Female exploitation

There were individual cases of women gaining in status and income in Stalin's time. But these were very much a minority and were invariably unmarried women or those without children. Married women with children carried a double burden. The great demand for labour that followed from Stalin's massive industrialisation drive required that women became essential members of the workforce. So, despite the theory about women being granted equality under Communism, in practice their obligations increased. They now had to fulfil two roles, as mothers raising the young to take their place in the new society and as workers contributing to the modernisation of the Soviet Union. This imposed great strains upon them. This was especially the case in the war of 1941–45. The terrible death toll of men at the front and the desperate need to keep the armaments factories running meant that women became indispensable (see Figure 6.1).

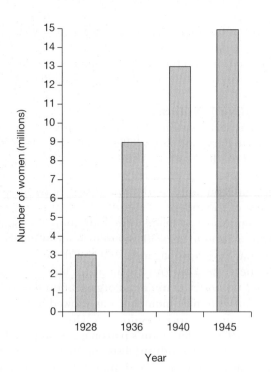

Figure 6.1: Number of women in the Soviet industrial workforce.

An equally striking statistic is that during the war over half a million women fought in the Soviet armed forces. However, rather than improving the status of women, this left them more vulnerable to mistreatment. It has come to light from recently opened Soviet records and the confessions of Red Army veterans that female soldiers were routinely sexually abused, especially by the senior officers.

The clear conclusion is that for all the Soviet talk of the liberation of women under Stalinism, the evidence suggests that they were increasingly exploited. They made a huge contribution to the Five-Year Plans and to wartime production. Without them the war effort could not have been sustained; by 1945 half of all Soviet workers were female. Yet they received no comparable reward. In fact, between 1930 and 1945 women's pay rates in real terms actually dropped. It is hard to dispute the conclusion of Geoffrey Hosking that 'the fruits of female emancipation became building blocks of the Stalinist **neopatriarchal** social system'.

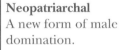

Key term

Neopatriarchal
A new form of male domination.

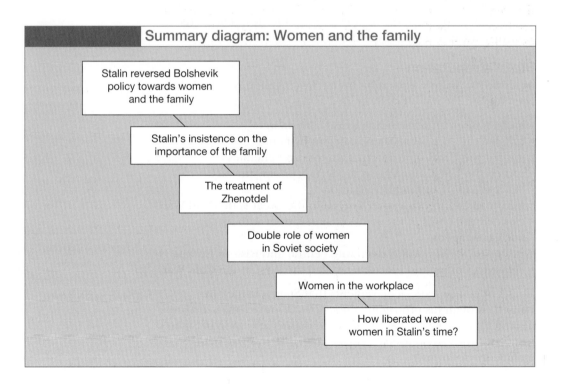

Summary diagram: Women and the family

Stalin reversed Bolshevik policy towards women and the family

Stalin's insistence on the importance of the family

The treatment of Zhenotdel

Double role of women in Soviet society

Women in the workplace

How liberated were women in Stalin's time?

7 | Stalin and Stalinism

The death of Stalin, 1953

Joseph Stalin's passing was a bizarre affair. At four o'clock on the morning of the first day of March 1953, after a night of heavy drinking with Party comrades, he retired alone to his study. Soon after, he collapsed. He lay unattended for over 12 hours on his divan bed, soaked in his own urine and unable to speak coherently. Even in his last hours he continued to terrify. His security guards knew something was wrong since he was not keeping to his regular routine. But they were afraid to act on their own initiative. They contacted the Kremlin, where the officials were equally frightened to do anything without authority. Eventually a number of doctors went in to see him. They reported that Stalin appeared to have had a stroke but they were too scared to recommend any particular treatment. In a bizarre development, the leading medical experts who had been imprisoned in the first stages of the doctors' purge (see page 74) had to be consulted. They gave their diagnosis from their cells. On the evidence they were given they suggested that Stalin's condition was very serious. And so it proved. He never recovered consciousness. Four days after first collapsing, Stalin was dead.

Stalin's reputation

At his death, Stalin's reputation in the Soviet Union could not have been higher. He was officially lauded as the great leader who had:

- made himself an outstanding world statesman
- fulfilled the socialist revolution begun by Lenin
- purged the USSR of its internal traitors and enemies
- turned the USSR into a great modern economy through collectivisation and industrialisation
- led the nation to victory over fascism in the Great Fatherland War
- elevated the USSR to the status of superpower with its own **nuclear weapons**
- extended Soviet borders deep into central and eastern Europe
- created a Communist bloc that rivalled the West in the **Cold War**.

These, of course, were achievements that Stalin claimed for himself through his propaganda machine. A more sober and more neutral estimate would have to include the negative side of Stalin's quarter-century of power. His legacy judged in this way might include the following.

At home
- Terror as a state policy.
- Authoritarian one-party rule by the CPSU.
- A single 'correct' ideology of Communism as dictated by Stalin.
- A misguided belief in the supremacy of Communist economic planning. Stalin's policy of collectivisation was so disruptive that it permanently crippled Soviet agriculture and left the USSR incapable of feeding itself.

Key question
How did Stalin's reputation stand at the time of his death?

Key terms

Nuclear weapons In 1949, Soviet scientists detonated the USSR's first atomic bomb.

Cold War The rivalry between the Soviet Union and the Western world between 1945 and 1991.

- His policy of enforced industrialisation achieved a remarkable short-term success but prevented the USSR from ever developing a truly modern economy.
- The abuse and deportations suffered by the ethnic peoples of the Soviet empire left them with a burning hatred that would eventually help to bring down the USSR.

Abroad

- A deep hostility towards the non-Communist world.
- The Cold War.
- International economic rivalry.
- Conflict with China for the leadership of world communism.

Key question
What was Stalin's record as national and Party leader?

Stalin's role as Soviet leader

It was the memory of Lenin's dominance of the Bolshevik Party that endured as the most powerful legacy of the 1917 Revolution. Reverence for the achievements of Lenin became a vital part of Communist tradition. It was Stalin's ability to suggest that he was continuing the work of Lenin that eased his own path to supremacy after 1924. Circumstances had made loyalty to the Party and loyalty to Lenin inseparable. Similarly, by the late 1920s, Stalin had succeeded in identifying his own authority with that of the rule of the Party. This made it extremely difficult for his fellow Communists to oppose him. To criticise Stalin was equivalent to doubting Lenin, the Party and the Revolution.

Stalin's intimate knowledge of the workings of the Secretariat aided him in his rise to power. By 1924 he had come to hold a number of important administrative positions, chief of which was the office of General Secretary of the CPSU. This left him ideally placed to control the appointment of members to the various posts within the Party's gift. Stalin became the indispensable link-man in the expanding system of Soviet government. Large numbers of Communist officials, the nomenklatura, owed their positions to Stalin's influence. They could not afford to be disloyal to him. This gave him a power-base which his rivals could not match. In the 1920s he was able to defeat all other contenders in the power struggle that followed Lenin's death.

The clear proof of how powerful Stalin had become was evident in the 1930s when he launched a series of purges of his real or imagined enemies in the government, the armed services and the Party. From then until his death in 1953, he exercised absolute authority over the Soviet Union.

Totalitarianism?

From time to time analysts have suggested that Stalin was not all-powerful – no one individual in a nation can be – and that his power depended on the willingness of thousands of underlings to carry out his orders and policies. In one obvious sense this must be true; no one person can do it all. It is for this reason that many historians are reluctant to use the word **totalitarianism** to describe his domination of the USSR.

Key term

Totalitarianism
Absolute state control.

What also worries them is that the term totalitarianism is too often used to describe the dominant European regimes of the 1920s and 1930s, Hitler's Nazi Germany and Stalin's Communist Russia, as if the authoritarian characteristics they shared, in particular an ideology that justified state terror, made them part of a common phenomenon. Their concern is that if these regimes are lumped together in this way, it blurs the real differences between them and diminishes the importance of the particular role of Stalin and the particular nature of the Soviet Union in the development of Stalinism.

However, it should be noted that there are other historians who, while not disputing the huge impact that Stalin had upon his country, point to other areas of significant development that occurred that did not depend on Stalin. This school of thought is sometimes referred to as the **bottom-up approach**. Writers in this school concentrate not so much on what Stalin did during the era he dominated the USSR, but on the reactions and attitudes of ordinary Soviet citizens. Sheila Fitzpatrick describes these historians as a 'new cohort' of post Cold War scholars who 'approach Stalinism like **anthropologists**, analysing practices, **discourses**, and rituals'. They were greatly helped in this by the opening of the former Soviet archives in the 1990s which allowed them to examine evidence previously closed to both Soviet and Western scholars.

Yet exciting though these new developments among the younger generation of historians are, the hard fact remains that whatever the attitudes of, and lives led by, ordinary Russians it was Stalin who gave the USSR its essential shape. Whatever the motives of those who carried out Stalin's policies, he was the great initiator. Little of importance took place in the USSR of which he did not approve. That is why some prominent historians, such as Robert Tucker, still speak of Stalinism as 'revolution from above', meaning that the changes that occurred under Stalin were directed by him from the top down.

Key terms

Bottom-up approach
The analysis of what was happening at the grass-roots level of society.

Anthropologists
Those who study the patterns of life of particular peoples and social groupings.

Discourses
The prevailing ideas and culture within a society.

De-Stalinisation

It is significant that the first sustained attack upon Stalinism as a personal form of autocratic rule came from within the Soviet Union itself. In February 1956, Nikita Khrushchev, the Soviet leader, delivered a dramatic 'Secret Report' to the 20th Congress of the CPSU. In a speech of remarkable range and venom, Khrushchev surveyed Stalin's career since the 1930s, exposing in detail the errors and crimes that Stalin had committed against the Party. Stalin had been guilty of 'flagrant abuses of power'. He had been personally responsible for the purges, 'those mass arrests that brought tremendous harm to our country and to the cause of socialist progress'.

Khrushchev quoted a host of names of innocent Party members who had suffered at Stalin's hands. Individual cases of gross injustice were cited and examples given of the brutality and torture used to extract confessions. Khrushchev's address was frequently

Key date

Khrushchev's 'Secret Report': February 1956. Although officially described as secret, details of Khrushchev's astounding revelations were soon known worldwide.

interrupted by outbursts of amazement and disbelief from the assembled members as he gave the details of the Stalinist terror.

The special term that Khrushchev used to describe the Stalinism that he was condemning was 'the cult of personality'. He explained that he meant by this that all the mistakes perpetrated in the Soviet Union since the 1930s had been a consequence of Stalin's lust for personal power, his 'mania for greatness'. With hindsight, it can be seen that Khrushchev's speech set in motion a debate about the character of Stalin and Stalinism that still continues.

The key debate

For decades scholars have been divided over the following issue:

> Was Stalin's despotism a logical progression from the authoritarianism of Lenin?

The reason why this was such a basic and important issue was that it went to the heart of the question as to whether Marxist Communism was the perfect social and political system that its adherents claimed it to be. In Communist belief, the justification for the 1917 Revolution led by Lenin was that it had been the first stage in a process that would culminate in the creation of the perfect society. If that process came to be corrupted, there would have to be an explanation. How could a perfect system become imperfect? To answer this, committed Communists set out to prove that Stalin had diverted Lenin's Revolution away from its true Marxist course. They claimed that the mistakes and terrors of the Stalin years were an aberration caused by Stalin's pursuit of his own personal power. Stalin's methods were not, therefore, a continuation of Lenin's policies but a departure from them; Stalinism was not a logical stage in the development of the Communist Revolution but a betrayal of it.

Alexander Solzhenitsyn, the leading dissident in Stalin's Russia, who underwent long years of imprisonment in the gulag, condemned the attempts to explain Stalinism in those terms. In 1974, he wrote that the concept of Stalinism as a distinct and discrete period of Soviet history was vital for Western Communists because:

> they shift onto it the whole bloody burden of the past to make their present position easier. It is no less necessary to those broad **Left-liberal circles** in the West which in Stalin's lifetime applauded highly coloured pictures of Soviet life.

> But close study of our [Soviet] modern history shows there never was any such thing as Stalinism ... Stalin was a very consistent and faithful – if also very untalented – heir to the spirit of Lenin's teaching.

Interestingly, Stalin refused to allow the term 'Stalinism' to be used, as if it represented something separate from traditional Communism. He always insisted that his task was to carry Lenin's

Key term

Left-liberal circles Westerners who were generally sympathetic towards Stalin and the USSR.

ideas to fruition. The principal aspects of his government of Soviet Russia – collectivisation, industrialisation, 'Socialism in One Country', cultural conformity – were officially described as 'Marxism–Leninism in action'.

From exile, Trotsky challenged this: he claimed that Stalin had laid his dead bureaucratic hand on Russia, thus destroying the dynamic revolution that Lenin had created. Isaac Deutscher and Roy Medvedev, both of whom suffered personally under Stalin, followed Trotsky in suggesting that Stalin had perverted the basically democratic nature of Leninism into a personal dictatorship.

However, Solzhenitsyn regarded Stalin as a 'blind, mechanical executor of Lenin's will' and stressed that the apparatus of the police state was already in place when Stalin took over. One-party rule, the secret police, the use of terror tactics, show trials – these were already in existence by 1924. Solzhenitsyn's analysis was backed by Western commentators such as Edward Crankshaw and Robert Conquest, who described Stalin's tyranny as simply a fully developed form of Lenin's essentially repressive creed of revolution.

Dmitri Volkogonov, the Russian biographer of the great trio who made the Russian Revolution, Lenin, Stalin and Trotsky, went further. He suggested that not only was there a direct line of continuity between Lenin and Stalin but that the methods they used to impose Communism on Russia meant that the Soviet Union could never become a truly modern state:

> The one-dimensional approach laid down by Lenin doomed Stalinism historically. By welding the Party organisation to that of the state, Stalinism gradually reshaped the legions of 'revolutionaries' into an army of bureaucrats. By adopting revolutionary methods to speed up the natural course of events, Stalinism ultimately brought the country to real backwardness.

Volkogonov also made the memorable suggestion that Stalinism, just as Leninism had, answered to a need in Russian society for faith in a great overarching idea. For him, Stalinism was one more example of the persistent feature that shaped Russian history:

> Stalinism, as the materialisation of Lenin's ideas, arose not only from the peculiarities of Russian history. Russia has always been a country of faith, the USSR no less, if only of the faith of anti-Christianity. Stalin was the embodiment of the system's drive for ideological faith.

Such interpretations were given powerful support by the opening up of the Soviet state archives in the 1990s following the fall of Communism and the break-up of the USSR. Robert Service, in his authoritative biography of Lenin published in 2004, pointed to an essential link between Lenin and Stalin. Building on the work of such analysts as Robert Tucker, Richard Pipes and Walter Laqueur, Service produced compelling evidence to establish his claim that Stalin, far from corrupting Lenin's policies, had fulfilled them. He confirmed that all the main features of the tyranny that Stalin exerted over the Soviet state had been inherited directly from Lenin.

Key question
What was Stalinism?

Defining Stalinism

As the foregoing section indicates, there will probably never be total agreement as to what Stalinism actually was, but the following list suggests some of the principal features of the system which operated during the quarter of a century in which Stalin had mastery over the USSR, and which need to be considered when working towards a definition.

- Stalin ran the USSR by a *bureaucratic* system of government.
- Stalin fulfilled the work begun by Lenin of turning revolutionary Russia into a *one-party state* in which all parties, other than the CPSU, were outlawed.
- Political and social control was maintained by *a terror system* whose main instruments were regular purges and show trials directed against the Party, the armed services and the people.
- A *climate of fear* was deliberately created so that no one could relax or challenge Stalin's policies.
- Stalin created *a command economy* with agriculture and industry centrally directed and no allowance made for local knowledge or initiative.
- As the only Communist state in existence, the USSR was *internationally isolated* in a largely capitalist, hostile world.
- Believing that Communism was based on scientific principles, Stalin insisted that the Soviet Union pursue the path of *socialist science.*
- Stalin's highly individual rule developed into a '*cult of personality*' which led to his becoming absolute in authority since he was regarded as the embodiment of the Communist Party and the nation.
- Stalin encouraged the development of an *elite nomenklatura,* officials who were loyal to Stalin because it was on his favour that their privileges depended. This stifled all criticism and made every official complicit in Stalin's crimes.
- Stalin created *a siege mentality* in the USSR. Even in peace time Stalin insisted that the Soviet people had to be on permanent guard from enemies within and hostile nations outside.
- Stalin was as intense *a nationalist* as ever the tsars had been. Notwithstanding its claim to be leading an international revolution, the Soviet Union under Stalin abandoned the active pursuit of revolution, making its priority instead the strengthening of the USSR as a nation.
- The Comintern, officially pledged to foment international revolution, spent its time defending the *interests of the USSR.*
- Stalin imposed his concept of '*revolution in one country*', a policy which subordinated everything to the interests of the Soviet Union as a nation. This involved the rejection of the Trotskyist alternative of '*permanent revolution*' which would have engaged the USSR in leading the movement for international revolution.

- Stalin's rule meant the suppression of any form of genuine democracy, since he operated on the principle, laid down by Lenin, of *democratic centralism*, which obliged members of the CPSU to accept uncritically and obey all orders and instructions handed down by the Party leaders.
- Under Stalin it was claimed the Soviet Union was a single-class nation. Recognition was given only to *the proletariat* in whose name and by whose authority Stalin held power. It was the role of the proletariat to destroy the remnants of all other classes.
- The USSR recognised only one correct and acceptable ideology, *Marxism–Leninism–Stalinism*. All other political, philosophical or religious belief systems were rejected.
- With the aim of creating a new type of human being, '*Homo sovieticus*', the Soviet Union under Stalin demanded cultural conformity in accordance with the notion of socialist realism.
- The enforcement of cultural conformity was achieved by the maintenance of strict forms of *censorship*.

Such features have been succinctly summarised by Robert Tucker in this definition:

Stalinism – born as the product of an unfinished proletarian revolution amidst a backward society encircled by a hostile capitalist environment – degenerated into a totally oppressive, dehumanizing ideology, expressing the interests of a gigantic bureaucratic elite.

One can predict with confidence that, despite all the subtle changes of approach that will undoubtedly come as historians continue to bring fresh insights to the study of Stalinism, this definition will continue to stand.

Some key books in the debate on Stalin and Stalinism:
Robert Conquest, *The Great Terror: Stalin's Purge of the Thirties* (Penguin, 1971)
Robert Conquest, *Harvest of Sorrow* (Macmillan, 1988)
Barbara Engel and Anastasia Posadskaya-Vanderbeck (eds), *A Revolution of their Own: Voices of Women in Soviet History* (University of Colorado Press, 1997)
Sheila Fitzpatrick, *Everyday Stalinism: Ordinary Life in Extraordinary Times: Soviet Russia in the 1930s* (OUP, 1999)
Sheila Fitzpatrick, *Stalinism: New Directions* (Routledge, 2000)
David L.E. Hoffman, *Stalinist Values: The Cultural Norms of Soviet Modernity* (Cornell University Press, 2003)
Walter Laqueur, *Stalin: The Glasnost Revelations* (Macmillan, 1990)
Roy Medvedev, *Let History Judge: The Origins and Consequences of Stalinism* (OUP, 1989)
Simon Sebag Montefiore, *Stalin: The Court of the Red Tsar* (Knopf, 2004)
Richard Pipes (ed.), *The Unknown Lenin: From the Soviet Archives* (Yale, 1996)

Robert Service, *Lenin: A Biography* (Macmillan, 2000)
Robert Service, *Stalin: A Biography* (Macmillan, 2004)
Alexander Solzhenitsyn, *The Gulag Archipelago* (Collins, 1974–78)
Robert C. Tucker, *Stalinism: Essays in Historical Interpretation* (Transaction Publishers, 1999)
Dmitri Volkogonov, *Lenin: Life and Legacy* (HarperCollins, 1994)
Dmitri Volkogonov, *Stalin: Triumph and Tragedy* (Weidenfeld and Nicolson, 1991)

Summary diagram: Stalin and Stalinism

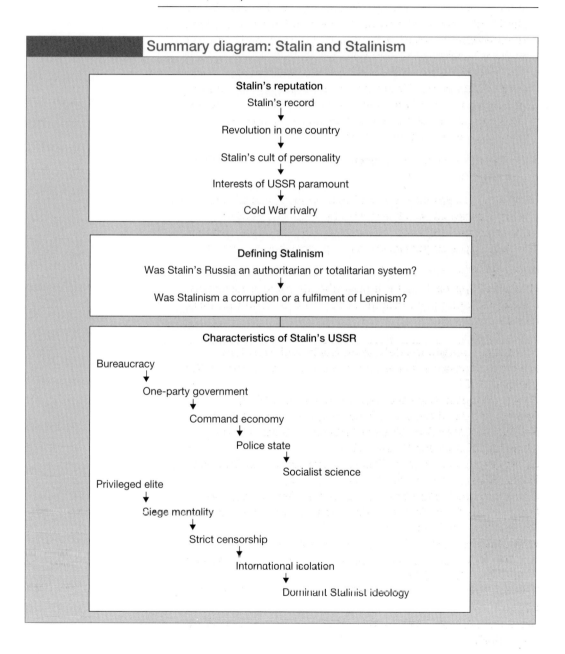

Study Guide: AS Questions

In the style of AQA

(a) Explain why Stalin transformed the education system in the USSR. (12 marks)

(b) 'Stalin was unsuccessful in his attempts to weaken the Orthodox Church between 1928 and 1941.' Explain why you agree or disagree with this view. (24 marks)

Exam tips

(a) In this question you need to cite a range of reasons and explain the links between them. Reasons might include:

- the need to modernise the USSR and increase standards of literacy
- to instil a greater sense of discipline which would be translated to adult life
- to extend knowledge of Marxist theory and Stalinist ideas (brainwashing)
- to provide the means whereby 'experts' (e.g. in medicine, science and administration) could be trained through an additional three years' non-compulsory schooling
- through the additional schooling to create a class of privileged administrators responsible and grateful to Stalin.

Don't forget that your answer should lead to a well-supported conclusion in which you identify the 'main' factor or factors.

(b) This question invites you to reflect on the position of the Church in the USSR under Stalin. You would need to consider the ways in which the authority and material power of the Church was attacked, particularly in 1928–29 during the period of collectivisation and the launching of the First Five-Year Plan and during the time of the purges in the later 1930s. The success of these campaigns would involve comment on the punishments given out to opponents, particularly priests, the halt to campaigns in the early thirties and comments on the continuing superstitious practices of the Russian peasantry. On the eve of war, religious belief was still strong and Stalin was to enlist religion in the subsequent surge of patriotic resistance. Remember you need to decide whether to agree or disagree with the quotation before beginning to write and should try to sustain an argument through your answer.

In the style of Edexcel

How far is it accurate to say that the position of women improved in Stalin's Russia?   (30 marks)

Exam tips

The cross-references are intended to take you straight to the material that will help you to answer the question.

This is a question requiring you to draw up a balance-sheet of changes that improved the position of women and those that did not, in order to reach an overall judgement. In order to note changes, you will first need to be clear about the position of women at the beginning of the period (page 122). You will also need to be clear about what criteria you are using when you claim an improved or a worsened position. On which side will you put material related to the headings below?

- The reversal of much Bolshevik social policy (pages 122–123)
- The role of women in the Party and women's organisations (pages 123–124)
- Women in the workforce and the armed forces (pages 97, 125) – opportunity or exploitation?
- Rates of pay (page 125)
- New family laws, 1944 (page 123)

So, what is your judgement? It is clear that the position of women changed in some ways. Do you think it improved?

Glossary

Anti-Comintern Pact Formed by the fascist nations, Germany, Italy and Japan, it carried a clear threat of a two-front attack on the Soviet Union's European and Far Eastern borders.

Anti-Semitism Hatred of the Jewish race.

Baltic States Estonia, Latvia and Lithuania.

Blat A system that operates through bribes, favours and connections.

Bolsheviks (Communists) The Bolsheviks, later known as Communists, began in 1903 as a breakaway group from the revolutionary Social Democrat Party (SDs).

Bottom-up approach Historical analysis of what was happening at the grass-roots level of society.

Bourgeoisie The exploiting capitalists.

Cadres Party members who were sent into factories and onto construction sites to spy and report back on managers and workers.

Capitalism The predominant economic system in Europe and the USA, based on private ownership and the making of profits – condemned by Marxists as involving the exploitation of the poor by the rich.

Capitalist methods of finance The system in which the owners of private capital (money) increase their wealth by making loans on which interest has to be paid later by the borrower.

Chimera A powerful but ultimately meaningless myth.

Cold War The rivalry between the Soviet Union and the Western world between 1945 and 1991.

Collective farms (*kolkhozy*) Co-operatives in which the peasants pooled their resources and shared the labour and the wages.

Collective security Nations acting together to protect individual states from attack.

Collectivisation The taking over by the Soviet state of the land and property previously owned by the peasants, accompanied by the requirement that the peasants now live and work communally.

Commissar Soviet term for high-ranking official or officer.

Commissar for Nationalities Minister responsible for liaising with the non-Russian national minorities.

Commissar of Enlightenment Equivalent to an arts minister.

Decree against Terrorist Acts (1st December Decree) This gave the NKVD limitless powers in pursuing enemies of the state and the Party.

Council of People's Commissars A cabinet of ministers, responsible for creating government policies.

CPSU The Communist Party of the Soviet Union.

Dacha   A country villa.

Deliver the votes   To use one's control of the Party machine to gain majority support in key votes.

Democratic centralism   The notion that true democracy in the Bolshevik Party lay in the obedience of the members to the instructions of the leaders.

Depression   A period of severe economic stagnation which began in the USA in 1929 and lasted throughout the 1930s. It affected the whole of the industrial world and was interpreted by Marxists as a sign of the final collapse of capitalism.

De-Stalinisation   The movement, begun by Khrushchev in 1956, to expose Stalin's crimes and mistakes.

Dialectic   The dynamic force that drives history along a predestined path.

Discourses   The prevailing ideas and culture within a society.

Economism   Putting the improvement of the workers' conditions before the need for revolution.

Factionalism   The forming within the Party of groups with a particular complaint or grievance.

February Revolution   The collapse of the tsarist monarchy following the abdication of Nicholas II, in February 1917.

'General Winter'   A popular way by which Russians referred to the help fierce winters traditionally gave them against an invader.

Geneva Convention   International agreements in 1906 and 1929 which had laid down the humane ways in which POWs should be treated.

Georgian   A tough race of people from the rugged land of Georgia in southern Russia.

Gigantomania   The worship of size for its own sake.

Gosplan   The government body responsible for national economic planning.

Grain procurements   Enforced state collection of fixed quotas of grain from the peasants.

Gulag   The vast system of prison and labour camps that spread across the USSR during the purges.

Holocaust   The genocide of six million Jews in occupied Europe between 1939 and 1945.

Homo sovieticus   A mock Latin term invented to describe the new 'Soviet man'.

Icons   Two-dimensional representations of Jesus Christ and the saints: the power and beauty of its icons is one of the great glories of the Orthodox Church.

Industrialisation   The introduction of a vast scheme for the building of factories which would produce heavy goods such as iron and steel.

Infant mortality   A calculation of the number of children who die per 100 or per 1000 of all those in a particular age group.

Intelligentsia   The group in society distinguished by their intellectual or creative abilities, e.g. writers, artists, composers, teachers.

Isvestiya   Official Soviet newspaper. Translates as 'The Times'.

Komsomol   The Communist Union of Youth.

Kremlin   The former tsarist fortress in Moscow that became the centre of Soviet government.

Kronstadt rising   A protest in 1921 by previously loyal workers and sailors at the Kronstadt naval base near Petrograd against the tyranny of Bolshevik rule – the rising was brutally suppressed by the Red Army acting under Trotsky's orders.

Kulaks   Rich peasants who had grown wealthy under NEP.

Labour Code   Severe regulations that had been imposed on the workers since 1918.

Laity   The ordinary people who attend church services.

League of Nations   The body set up in 1919 with the aim of resolving all international disputes.

Left Communists   Party members who wanted NEP abandoned.

Left-liberal circles   Westerners who were generally sympathetic towards Stalin and the USSR.

Lend-lease programme   The importing by the Soviet Union of war materials from the USA with no obligation to pay for them until after the war, an extension of the system by which earlier in the war the USA had provided aid to Britain.

Leningrad (Petrograd)   The city was renamed in Lenin's honour three days after his death.

Luftwaffe   The German air force.

Marxists   Believers in the theories of the German revolutionary Karl Marx (1818–83), who taught that history was predetermined and took the form of a series of violent class struggles culminating in the victory of the proletariat over all its enemies.

May Day ('Labour Day')   1 May, traditionally regarded as a special day for honouring the workers and the achievements of socialism.

Mein Kampf   'My Struggle', the title of Hitler's autobiographical book, written in the 1920s and regarded as the Nazi bible.

Mensheviks   A Marxist party that had split from the Bolsheviks when the SD Party broke up in 1903.

Neopatriarchal   A new form of male dominance.

Neo-traditionalism   A return to customary, established ways of doing things.

Nepmen   Those farmers and traders who were considered to have unfairly exploited the New Economic Policy, introduced by Lenin in 1921, to line their own pockets.

NKVD   The state secret police, a successor of the *Cheka* and a forerunner of the KGB.

Nomenklatura   The Soviet 'establishment' – a privileged elite of officials who ran the Party machine.

Normandy landings   The opening of a second front in Europe by a large-scale American–British invasion in western France in 1944.

Nuclear weapons   In 1949, Soviet scientists detonated the USSR's first atomic bomb.

'October deserters'   Those Bolsheviks who in October 1917, believing that the Party was not yet strong enough, had advised against a Bolshevik rising.

OGPU   Succeeded the *Cheka* as the state security force; in turn it became the NKVD and then the KGB.

Operation Bagration   The 58-day battle in 1944 that cost a combined total of 765,000 Russian and German casualties.

Operation Citadel   The German code name for the Kursk campaign in 1943.

Orgburo The Workers' and Peasants' Inspectorate.

Orthodox Church The official state religion of tsarist Russia.

'Packets' Privileges and special benefits.

Panzer Fast armoured tank units.

Paranoia A persecution complex which gives the sufferer the conviction that he is surrounded by enemies intent on harming him.

Party card The official CPSU document granting membership and guaranteeing privileges to the holder. It was a prized possession in Soviet Russia.

Patronage The right to appoint individuals to official posts in the Party and government.

Pogrom State-organised persecution involving physical attacks upon Jews and the destruction of their property.

Politburo The inner cabinet of the ruling Central Committee of the CPSU.

Political correctness The requirement that people conform to a prescribed set of opinions when expressing themselves, to show that they have accepted the ideology of the leaders of society.

Political expediency Pursuing a course of action with the primary aim of gaining a political advantage.

Pravda The truth, title of a Bolshevik newspaper.

Pragmatic Deciding policy on the basis of fact and circumstance rather than theory.

Proletariat The revolutionary working class destined to achieve ultimate triumph in the class war.

Proletkult Proletarian culture.

Provisional Government Drawn from the remnants of the Duma (the Russian parliament which ended in 1917), it attempted to govern Russia between February and October 1917.

Purges In theory, a means of purifying the Communist Party; in practice, a system of terror by which first Lenin and later Stalin removed anyone they regarded as a threat to their authority.

Quasi-religious faith A conviction so powerful that it has the intensity of religious belief.

Red Army Between 1918 and 1920, Trotsky, as War Commisar, turned a ramshackle assortment of veterans and untrained recruits into a formidable three million-strong force to defend the Revolution.

Red Terror The brutal methods adopted by Lenin to destroy opposition and resistance to the Bolsheviks.

Revolution from below The Communist claim that the 1917 Revolution had been a genuine rising of the people rather than a power grab by the Bolsheviks.

Right Communists Party members who wanted NEP to continue.

Russian famine, 1921 So severe that Lenin had had reluctantly to accept some $60 million worth of aid from the American Relief Association.

Ryutin group Followers of M. N. Ryutin, a Right Communist, who had published an attack on Stalin, describing him as 'the evil genius who had brought the Revolution to the verge of destruction'.

Salient An area that protrudes into the enemy's lines forming a bulge.

'Second revolution'   Term used by Stalin to describe his crash programme to modernise the Soviet economy.

Secretariat (Apparat)   A form of civil service, responsible for carrying out government policies.

Seminaries   Training colleges for priests.

Show trials   Special public court hearings meant as propaganda exercises in which the accused, whose guilt is assumed, are paraded as enemies of the people.

Socialist realism   A form of representational art which the people can understand and relate to their own lives.

Soviet Union of Writers   The body having authority over all published writers. Under Stalin's direction it had the right to ban or censor any work of which it disapproved.

Soviets   Councils of workers and soldiers, which the Bolsheviks came to dominate and in whose name they carried out the October Revolution.

SRs   Socialist Revolutionaries, the largest of the revolutionary parties in Russia until outlawed by the Bolsheviks after 1917.

State farms (*sovkhozy*)   Contained peasants working directly for the state, which paid them a wage.

'Storming'   An intensive period of work to meet a highly demanding set target.

Subsistence level   The bare minimum required to sustain life.

Tax in kind   The surrendering by the peasant of a certain amount of his produce, equivalent to a fixed sum of money.

'Total theatre'   An approach which endeavours to break down the barriers between actors and audience by revolutionary use of lighting, sound and stage settings.

Totalitarianism   Absolute state control.

Triumvirate   A ruling or influential bloc of three persons.

Tuberculosis   A wasting disease which was especially prevalent in Russia.

United Opposition (New Opposition)
The group who called for an end to NEP and the adoption of a rapid industrialisation programme.

Urals   The mountain range dividing European Russia from its Asian east.

USSR   The Union of Soviet Socialist Republics – the formal title of Bolshevik Russia, adopted in 1922 and often shortened to the Soviet Union.

Utopian   Belief in the attainability of a perfect society.

Versailles Settlement   The peace treaty of 1919 which redrew the map of Europe.

Vozhd   Russian term for a supreme leader, equivalent to *der Führer* in German.

War of attrition   A grinding conflict in which each side hopes to win by wearing the other down.

Whites   Counter-revolutionaries, including members of parties outlawed by the Bolsheviks, and monarchists, looking for a tsarist restoration.

White Sea Canal   Linking Leningrad with the White Sea; built predominantly by forced labour.

Yalta and Potsdam Conferences Held respectively in February and July 1945, these were the major gatherings of the victorious Allies concerned with drawing the map of the post-war world.

Yezhovschina The period of terror directed at ordinary Soviet citizens in the late 1930s and presided over by Yezhov, the head of the NKVD.

Zhenotdel The Women's Bureau of the Communist Party.

Index